ENVIRONMENT AND INTEGRATED CHILD DEVELOPMENT SERVICES

BOOKS BY THE SAME AUTHOR

1. Primitive, Folk and Modern Medicine-A selected bibliography with special reference to community nutrition. (1973) Published by CARE.
2. Folk and Modern Medicine-A North Indian Case Study (1977). New Asian Publishers. Foreword by Dr. P.N. Chhuttani.
3. Dais-The Traditional Birth Attendants in Village India. (1980) New Asian Publishers.
4. Psychosocial Factors Affecting Family Welfare-A study of 'Leaders' in Punjab and Haryana (with associates) (1982). Published by Indian Council of Medical Research, New Delhi. Foreword by Dr. I.C. Pathak.
5. Child and Maternal Health Services in Rural India. The Narangwal Experiment (1983) (with associates) World Bank Publication. The Johns Hopkins University Press, Baltimore, USA. Foreword by Dr. Ashok Mitra.
6. Women and Family Planning (1984), Sterling Publishers.
7. Services and Psychosocial Research in Family Planning (1984) (edited with associates). Published by Indian Council of Medical Research. Foreword by Dr. V. Ramalingaswamy.
8. Child Health, Nutrition and Family Planning, 1984 (edited with associates). Published by Indian Council of Medical Research. Foreword by Dr. V. Ramaligaswamy.
9. Sociocultural Determinants of Fertility. 1986. (edited with associates). Published by Indian Council of Medical Research. Foreword by Dr. V. Ramalingaswamy.
10. Women's Accesibility to Health and Family Planning (1987) (edited with associates). Published by Indian Council of Medical Research, New Delhi Foreword by Dr. A.S. Paintal.
11. Primary Health Care and Traditional Medical Practitioners (1988) Sterling Publishers. Foreword by Dr. Charles Leslie.
12. The Pill Users : A Study in an Urban Setting (1990) Capital Publishers.

ENVIRONMENT AND INTEGRATED CHILD DEVELOPMENT SERVICES

D.N. KAKAR

UPPAL PUBLISHING HOUSE
NEW DELHI-110002

UPPAL PUBLISHING HOUSE
3, Ansari Road, Daryaganj New Delhi-110 002

First Published 1992
ISBN 81-85565-12-0

Printed in India
Published by B.S. Uppal, for Uppal Publishing, House
New Delhi-110 002 and Printed at R.N. Printers
1/2208, Shanti Building, Shahdara, Delhi-110 032

Preface

This book is about implementation of the integrated child development services (ICDS) scheme in a poverty environment. Nowhere is the economic slight of the Indian child more apparent than among the weakest sections of our society such as the scheduled castes and the backward classes. Poverty in the villages and slums of Chandigarh means a life full of despair and powerlessness. It means an high incidence of childhood malnutrition and illness. It means living in crowded homes, surrounded by unhygienic conditions. It means little or no health care, no opportunity for pre-school education and no help for overcoming nutritional deficiencies. The poverty environment is generally a constricted one. Children raised in such an environment are bound to have little experience outside their immediate neighbourhoods. The ICDS scheme is meant to help such children. It is unique in several respects. Firstly, it is the only scheme that tends to integrate three major components of human resource development, namely health, nutrition, and education. Secondly, it is multi-sectoral. Thirdly, lt is primarily Indian. Fourthly, it is almost entirely funded by national sources. Fifthly, it is futuristic in orientation. Sixthly, it is meant for the poorest sections of the society, especially the vulnerable segments. And lastly, it functions under the leadership of a galaxy of Indian scientists. Yet, it can acqnire a good image only if the community takes the 'front seat' in its implementation. Lack of community participation is largely responsible for its slow progress. This could be abundantly clear from our study. However, we have tried to highlight the strengths as well as the weaknesses of the ICDS scheme. We hope the findings of our study would be useful to the policy makers, health administrators, medical and social science researchers and others concerned with the implementation of this scheme.

In carrying out this research work, I have been helped by so many people that here I can only mention the few upon whose help and cooperation I have depended a great deal. I am gratefull to Dr. B.N.S. Walia, Director, Postgraduate Institute of Medical Education and Research, Chandigarh, for his encouragement and help in my academic pursuits. I am also gratefull to D. P.N. Chhuttani, a former Director of the PGI, for his encouragement. I am thankfull to Dr. R.C. Mahajan, for his help. My thanks are also due to Dr. Indu Gupta for her help and cooperation. Mrs. S. Samuel, Principal college of Nursing, and Mrs. Saroj Sharma have always been a great help in our research work. I am indebted to Dr. Suksham Chopra for her painstaking effort in helping me complete this study. She has ably assisted me in data collection, analysis and interpretation. I am highly appreciative of the effort of my other colleagues in the Department, namely, Dr. A. Singh, Dr. Lily Agarwal, Dr. Alka Saigal, Dr. Vikas Bhatia, Dr. Kartik and Mrs. Kulwant Kaur. I am indebted to several other professional colleagues of mine especially Dr. Charles Leslie of Newark, USA, Dr. Akrele of WHO, Geneva, and Dr. Beatrix Bfleiderer of Germany. I am particularly grateful to Mr. Sayal, for going through the manuscript. My son, Shivendra (Sammy) has offered his critical comments on the draft and my wife, Indira, has tried to rectify many mistakes in it. Finally. I must thank the anganwadi workers for having shared with me their experiences about the ICDS scheme.

March, 1992 D.N. KAKAR
Chandigarh (India)

Contents

1

Introduction to ICDS

What is the ICDS scheme all about ? The history of the ICDS scheme is fairly simple to recall. It was launched on the auspicious occasion of the 106th birth anniversary of Mahatma Gandhi, the Father of the Nation, purely on an experimental basis in 33 administrative blocks. The launching of the scheme was preceded by a careful examination of the existing health and developmental programmes for women and children in the country. By March 1990, as many as 2, 197 blocks, of a total of 5147 development blocks, were covered under this scheme.[1,2] In addition, there were 227 ICDS projects in 2 urban areas. The scheme was started in recognition of the grim background of high infant mortality rate, high level of childhood morbidity rate, high incidence of childhood malnutrition and nutrition-related diseases, temporary or irreversible disabilities, and low literacy rate—all indicators of a slow progress of development. And it was in recognition of the fact that the fruits of development had an uneven distribution in our country. Inequality of opportunities had deprived large sections of women and children of the benefits due to them. No wonder, their quality of life is far inferior to that of their privileged counterparts. Since children are an investment in the future, we have to educate them and provide them ample opportunities for development—physical, social and mental. And we have to reduce the existing high rate of childhood morbidity and mortality—a major stumbling block in our social and economic progress[3,4]. The ICDS scheme, therefore, was an appropriate response to the needs of millions of children in our country who lived in poor social, economic and environmental conditions which hindered their development. And the scheme did recognise the important linkage between the welfare of the child and the welfare of the mother. Moreover, the scheme went beyond the existing health and education systems to reach out to children, pregnant women and nursing mothers, especially those belonging to the weaker sections of the society. And it gave the highest importance to preschool age so as to lay a strong enough foundation for the integrated development of children. The objectives of the ICDS scheme were : (i) to improve the nutritional and health status of children in the age group 0-6 years ; (ii) to lay the foundation for proper psychological, physical and social development of the child ; (iii) to reduce the incidence of mortality, morbidity, malnutrition and school drop-outs ; (iv) to achieve effective coordination of policy and implementation amongst the various departments to promote child development ; and (v) to enhance the capability of the mother to look after the normal health and nutritional needs of the child through proper nutrition and health education.[5] A package of services was provided under this scheme. This was based primarily on the consideration that the overall impact will be much larger if the different services develop in an integrated manner as the efficiency of a particular service depends upon the support it receives from the related services'. It was rightly assumed that the provision of supplementary nutrition would not improve the health of the child if he continued to be exposed to diarrhocal disease and other infections or unprotected drinking water supply. The package of services, therefore, was not created in a vacuum. On the contrary, the selection of services was done with utmost care on the basis of four vital considerations ; (i) need for the services ; (ii) inter-dependence and mutual support relationships ; (iii) cost ; and (iv) administrative feasibility. The six services of this integrated package were : (i) non-formal preschool education; (ii) immunization; (iii) health check-ups; (iv) supplementry nutrition ; (v) medical referral services ; and (vi) nutrition and health education for women. These services were supplemented with functional literacy for adult women. Simultaneously, efforts were made for the convergence of the rural drinking water supply programme in the ICDS project areas. Besides, stress was laid on applied nutrition activities like local production and consumption of nutritious food.[6] The services were delivered to the beneficiaries in a planned way. And the services were provided to children below the age of six years. The criterion of age was decided on the consideration that preschool age is a definite phase in the development of the child and that earlier childhood is more crucial for child's development. Earlier childhood was, therefore, reclassified into different age groups so that services could be delivered in accordance with the differential needs of the children. Also, in recognition of the fact that the mother played a key role in the physical, psychological, and social development of the child, nursing and expectant mothers were included in the scheme. It was felt that ultimately women of 15-45 years will have to be brought within the ambit of the ICDS scheme. The focal point of the convergence of these services was the anganwadi or preschool child centre, located within the village. Each anganwadi was run by an anganwadi worker (AWW) with the assistance of a helper. An anganwadi was supposed to cover a population of 1000 in rural and urban areas and 700 in tribal areas. Regarding health check-ups, all children and expectant and nursing mothers were to be examined, at regular intervals by the lady health visitor (LHV) and auxiliary nurse midwife (ANM), who were supposed to diagnose minor ailments and distribute simple medicines. This way they were expected to provide a link between the village and primary health care subcentre. All children in the project area were to be immunized against six commonly prevalent illnesses—diptheria, whooping cough, tetanus, poliomyelitis, tuberculosis and measles. Pregnant women were also to be immunized against tetanus. For supplementary nutrition, all families in the community were to be surveyed to identify the poorest children below the age of six as well as expectant and nursing mothers. They were to be distributed food for 300 days a year. The food was to be prepared at the anganwadi—either a hot meal or a ready-to-eat snack containing the same basic ingredients. Special care was to be taken to reach children below the age of three and to encourage parents and siblings to bring them to the anganwadi for feeding. By providing 300 calories a day to children under six years, it was felt, that the calorie gap between the national average intake of 810 calories and the required 1200 calories per day will be bridged. In addition, specific micro-nutrients were to be supplied to overcome regional or individual deficiencies such as Vitamin A for blindness, iron for anaemia and iodated salt for iodine deficiency disorders like stunted growth, physical disability and mental retardation. All children below the age of six were also to be weighed or measured for height periodically. Weight/height for age growth charts were to be maintained at the anganwadi to identify malnourshed children so that those suffering from severe malnutrition (Grades III and IV) could be given special supplementary nutrition and acute cases referred to the health centres for prompt medical attention. In addition, all children between the ages of three and five years were to attend the anganwadi three hours a day. The pre-school education was meant to stimulate and satisfy the curiosity of young children. They were to be taught songs and games with the help of toys produced from inexpensive, locally available materials. Also, non-formal training in nutrition and health education was to be organized at the anganwadi for mothers and pregnant women. For this purpose, all women between 15-45 were invited but priority was to be given to pregnant and nursing mothers and mothers of children who suffered from repeated illness and malnutrition. Several methods were to be employed to reach mothers such as home visits by the AWW, special campaigns, informal gatherings and audio visual presentations.[7] The ICDS projects were to be selected on the basis of need. For instance, in rural areas, selection of projects was to be made on the basis of factors such as (i) areas predominantly inhabited by tribes, particularly backward tribes; (ii) backward areas; (iii) droughtprone areas (iv) areas inhabited predominantly by the scheduled castes; (v) nutritionally deficient areas; and (vi) areas poor in development of social services. On the other hand, in the selection of wards in urban areas, for urban projects, priority was to be given to the (i) location of slums and (ii) areas predominantly inhabited by the scheduled castes. The selection of project areas was to be co-ordinated with the programme of the Health and Family Welfare Ministry to strengthen the primary health set-up and with the programme for protected water supply of the Ministry of Works and Housing. In fact, it was to be coordinated with several other programmes of different departments in the centre and the state.

The ICDS scheme had been classified as a centrally sponsored programme. However, it was being implemented through the State Government with 100 percent financial assistance from the Central Government for inputs other than supplementary nutrition. It was stated that the states were expected to provide funds for supplementary nutrition under Minimum Needs Programme in the States sector. The Central Social Welfare Board, voluntary organizations, local bodies and Panchayati Raj Institutions were to be actively involved in this programme for speedy implementation. The intention was to entrust the running of anganwadis to voluntary organizations, local bodies and Panchayati Raj institutions by giving them grant-in-aid. Since the scheme was based on the strategy of an intersectoral approach to the development of children, it was felt that coordination of the efforts of different Ministeries and departments would be required at all levels. For instance, the Ministry of Health and Family Welfare was to indicate the norms of the health services to be attained in the project areas. And the PHC and Subordinate health infrastructure were to provide (i) health check-up, (ii) referral services: and (iii) immunization to the beneficiaries in the ICDS areas. The implementation of the programme at the block level was entrusted to Child Development Project Officer (CDPO). The CDPO was expected (i) to provide a link between the ICDS and government administration; (ii) to secure anganwadi premises; (iii) to provide supervision to four supervisors and 100 anganwadis; (iv) to identify beneficiaries and ensure supply of food to centre; and flow of health services and (v) monitor programme, and send reports to the government. The CDPO's assistant—a Mukhya Savika—was to (i) supervise 20-25 anganwadis (ii) act as mentor to anganwadi workers, (iii) assist in record keeping, and organising community visits to health personnel and (iv) provide on the job training to anganwadi workers. However, the anganwadi worker was supposed to be the sheet-anchor of the ICDS programme. She was expected to perform a multiplicity of roles in the capacity of a multipurpose change agent. She was to be selected from the community. She was to provide direct link to children and mothers. Besides, she was to assist the CDPO in conducting surveys of communities and beneficiaries. She was also responsible for organizing non-formal education as well as for providing health and nutrition education to mothers. Her other roles were: (i) providing assistance to PHC staff in the delivery of health services; (ii) maintenance of records of immunization, feeding and preschool attendance; doing liaison work with block administration, local schools, health staff and community and providing assistance in other community-based activities such as family planning. Thus she was one functionary on whose motivation, knowledge, skills and actions depended the future of the entire ICDS programme. The ICDS programme was being monitored at regular intervals. The emphasis was on 'functional monitoring' so that corrective actions could be taken in time. The task of monitoring and evaluation was given to the health and social welfare sectors. In this regard, a significant development took place, in 1982, when the Department of Women and Child Development installed a word processor. This helped in the compilation of quarterly monitoring reports from the CDPO. However, of late, the word processor has been replaced by micro-computers. And this has greatly helped in assessing the performance of the scheme in various States and Union Territories. With the timely availability of reports, the concerned states and Union Territories could initiate necessary corrective action.[8] The Central Technical Committee's Cell at the AIIMS had also started computerized processing of the monthly monitoring reports related to health staff, orientation training in the health sector, supplies of medical and health items, vital events like birth rate and infant mortality rate and morbidity data. Actually the main ICDS team of the Social Welfare Department comprised the anganwadi workers (AWWs), the supervisors (MSs), and the Child Development Project Officer (CDPO) This team was to interact with a team of medical officers, the lady health visitors and female health workers from nearby primary health centres and subcentres to implement the ICDS scheme. The anganwadi workers were to receive three months basic training followed by monthly visits from a medical team and subsequent refresher courses. There were 292 AWWs' training centres and 20 Middle level training centres including three CDPOs' training centres. As many as 102 senior faculty members representing 83 medical colleges had been engaged in delivering orientation and refresher courses to the district and block level health functionaries.

By march 1990, as many as 2,21,422 anganwadi workers, 12,678 supervisors and 2,778 CDPOs were imparted training. In addition, a total of 21,457 health functionaries were provided orientation training.[9] It was revealed that since April 1988, the Central Technical Committee at the All India Institute of Medical Sciences had adopted an innovative approach of integrated training for MOs and CDPOs of the ICDS projects, under the National Programme for mother and child development by replacing the earlier orientation and training programme. The curiculla for training/orientation/continued education were being constantly reviewed in the light of field experience. As the main stress was on practical training, manuals and a guide-book had been published on diarrhoea. The data originating at the anganwadis, were, therefore, available for comparing the performance at the state and national levels. All these are highly visible signs of hope. Yet, it is necessary to be watchful and see how the programme is functioning at the field level. The true reality of the field situation should be known. Our effort here would be to reveal this reality with the help of our studies, done at the macro and micro levels.

REFERENCES

1. Integrated Child Development Services (1990) Department of Women and Child Development, Ministry of Social Welfare, Government of India.

2. Integrated Nutrition Education—A Handbook, Food and Nutrition Board, Department of Food and Civil Supplies, Government of India, 1991.

3. The State of World's Children (1991), United Nations Children's Fund (UNICEF), Oxford University Press.

4. Kielmann, et al (1983) Child and Maternal Health Services in Rural India. The Narangwal Experiment. World Bank Research Publication, the Johns Hopkins University Press, Baltimore, USA.

5. Integrated Child Development Services (1990) op, cit.

6. Integrated Child Development Services Scheme (Revised) (1982). Ministry of Social Welfare, Government of India, New Delhi.

7. ICDS—Integrated Child Development Services in India (1984), UNICEF, New Delhi, India.

8. ICDS—Integrated Child Development Services (1990) Department of Women and Child Development, Ministry of Welfare, Government of India.

9. ICDS—Integrated Child Development Services (1990) Op. Cit.

2

Social and Health Environment of Chandigarh and ICDS

Chandigarh, named after 'Chandi', the goddess of power can best be described as a city of constrasts. As a uni-district territory, Chandigarh came into being on first November, 1966. This became possible as a result of trifurcation of the erstwhile Punjab State into Punjab, Haryana and Himachal Pradesh. Chandigarh is presently the capital of both Punjab and Haryana. Administratively, Chandigarh functions under the Central Government. Way back in 1971, Chandigarh had a population of 2,18,743. But in 1991, the Union Territory of Chandigarh had recorded a population of 6,40,725 (3,57,411 males and 2,83,314 females). Chandigarh today is coping with tremendous economic development and industrialization that has improved the lot of many women and children but has by-passed others. The commercialism has raised living standards, but socially and culturally Chandigarh has to go a long way. Its huge migrant population (over 70%) has kept the city somewhat fragmented. There is little mixing of its white-collar workers with blue-collar workers. Two decades ago, one could walk the streets of Chandigarh without seeing too many vehicles on the road. Today, one has to face heavy traffic on practically all roads of the city, thanks to its manifold expansion of population.

The majority of people of Chandigarh have migrated from other states. Many of them came in search of jobs and found it convenient to join various occupations. A large number of students also came to Chandigarh for joining various professional courses like medicine, engineering and architecture. Lack of economically productive occupations, coupled with shortage of amenities like medical care and communication, may have compelled families out of their natural habitat to migrate to Chandigarh. When thousands of young men and women migrate to urban areas in search of employment, they loosen themselves from the emotional support they had been getting from their communities. The worst affected are disabled children who are in greater need of emotional support from their families of orientation. The lack of emotional support affects the members of a family, especially children, more adversely than does the lack of economic support.

Erosion of the joint family has had its own adverse effects on the lives of many youngsters in Chandigarh. Those living in nuclear families no longer have the same advantage which their counterparts representing the joint families had. Youngsters in a joint family had no dearth of occasions exposing them to the basic values which helped them direct their lives along channels which were traditionally acceptable and conducive to the family goals. Among the juveniles in Chandigarh, one does not find much evidence of such influence. Today, many a juvenile in Chandigarh looks beyond the customary horizon for non-religious values. Possession of luxury items, like a motorcar or a two-wheeler is something they can not resist. And high incidence of traffic accidents, violence and regression, involving men and women representing opulent sections of the society, in particular, is nothing but a natural consequence of this life style.

The majority of people in Chandigarh speak Hindi or Punjabi though other languages like Bengali, Malayalam, Tamil Urdu and English are also spoken. The majority of the population consists of Hindus and Sikhs. Other religious groups like Christian, Muslims and Budhists, constitute a tiny minority.

Twenty years ago, one saw few women driving four-wheelers or two-wheelers in the city. Today, one sees hundreds of working women reaching their destinations in self-driven four-wheelers and two-wheelers. These are indeed mind-boggling changes and provide an evidence of the influence of modernization. Moreover, today, there is hardly a destination in Chandigarh's rural and urban areas which cannot be reached by a bus or a two-wheeler. Many new houses and buildings including hotels have sprouted in different sectors of the city. Much of the building boom has occurred in recent years. No doubt, inflation has risen a great deal. It has hit practically all categories of office-goers including academics and students. Microwave ovens and washing machines have not yet made their way into the average Chandigarh household but television has. Women and children of Chandigarh.s opulent classes, in particular, are in constant touch with the outside world. Many of them have acquired a new level of sophistication and a taste for more and better consumer goods. They have moved out of household work into educational institutions, factories, trades and services.

Basically, the working class women in Chandigarh can be divided into three different groups—skilled, semi-skilled and unskilled workers. Differences in economic and prestige rewards are linked to this hierarchy of skills. The skilled women like doctors and teachers enjoy higher wages, more valuable fringe benefits, greater job security, and higher prestige than semi-skilled and unskilled workers. A recent classifieation of working women shows that a majority of them belonged to Class III (Non-gazetted officers)[2]. Among the working women in Chandigarh, we find a plurality of status and skill groups. We also find that those in the higher income group exhibit a tendency to guard their wage differentials against claims for pay increases by the less-skilled. In general, women who are engaged in blue-collar occupations, despite their lower earnings, worked longer hours than their white-collar counterparts. Despite the increasing stress on primary health care, many female health workers like lady health uisitors, (LHVs) and auxiliary nurse-midwives (ANMs) find practically no opportunity for promotion and their pay structures have not included sufficient incremental increases. Their career mobility, therefore, is greatly restricted. However, the same is not true of their counterparts belonging to higher occupational groups. It may be worthwhile to mention that in China as well as in Tanzania, great stress has been laid on the career mobility of lower and intermediate level of health functionaries. Presently, the Aga Khan University in Karachi, Pakistan, is experimenting with new roles for such health functionaries. Again in Chandigarh, the women engaged in white-collar occupations generally enjoy higher standards of health as compared to their blue-collar counterparts. They invariably have lower rates of maternal mortality, pre-natal mortality and postnatal mortality; a lower incidence of long-standing illnesses and a longer life expectancy. They also have higher levels of educational attainment. Moreover, children representing white-collar backgrounds generally obtain higher educational qualifications than the children representing blue-collar backgrounds. Measured in terms of material possessions, like television sets, refrigerators, and automobiles, white-collar women workers enjoy a superior quality of life than that of their blue-collar counterparts. Their houses are more spacious and hygienic. Their jobs are more secure and they work shorter hours : they can spend more time with their children looking after their health. But the same is not true of women engaged in blue-collar occupations.

During 1991, sex ratio in Chandigarh was 793 females for 1000 males, while the national figure was 933 in 1981. The adverse sex ratio in Chandigarh is atributable to a number of factors. Firstly, it may be because of the universal biological phenomenon of less number of females. Secondly, it may have been due to culturally determined and socially sanctioned preference for male children, resulting in the neglect of female babies. This is well reflected by our case studies of female malnourished children in rural Punjab.[8] Thirdly, the disparity in sex ratio may have also been due to differential mortality rates, particularly maternal mortality rate in child bearing age of 15-44. Kerala is the only state in India which has a favourble sex ratio. Imbalance in the sex ratio in Chandigarh has led to certain social consequences including the problem of finding suitable spouses within approachable geographical boundries. In rural areas of Chandigarh, the lowest sex ratio has been recorded in villages with less than 200 population, followed by those with a population of 500 or more.

In the villages of Chandigarh, as elsewhere in the country-side in India, members of the scheduled castes and backward classes still live on the outskirts. However, it must be clarified that today they are not as segregated as they were a few decades ago. But because of inequalities, they are still far behind their better of counterparts. Though the scheduled caste people in Chandigarh constitute only 14.09% of the population, most of them have not had either a taste of power or wealth.

Needless to say that inequalities of wealth are linked to those of prestige and power.

In the present economy of Chandigarh, the landowners have much greater power and prestige than those who are landless. Members of rich and poor classes and castes have different identities, interests and life styles. Thus they differently enjoy or suffer the unequal distribution of rewards. Social stratification, therefore, is just one from of social inequality to which members of lower classes and castes are subjected. In a stratification system, the position of a scheduled caste female child may have important effects on many areas of life. It may enhance or reduce her life chances of obtaining things defined as desirable or avoiding things defined as undesirable. For instance, a woman's life chances include everything from the chance to stay alive during the first year after birth to the chance to remain healthy and grow well. A comparison of the scheduled caste women with their non-scheduled caste counterparts could give one an idea about the effect of stratification system on their life chances. For instance, the infant mortality rate was found to be much higher among the scheduled caste women than among the non-scheduled caste women in selected north Indian villages. Also, the proportion of the scheduled caste mothers dying during birth was relatively higher than that of their non-scheduled caste mothers. Moreover, fewer scheduled castes girls acquired educational qualifications than their non-scheduled caste counterparts. Thus their chances for employment were relatively reduced. Normally, a stratification system is accompanied by a set of beliefs. For instance some, people representing the upper strata in Chandigarh believe that social inequalities to which the scheduled caste women have been subjected are biologically based. Some of them even claim biological superiority over those belonging to the lower strata or the scheduled castes. Actually, they often see this as the basis for their dominance. Now, howsoever defective their preception may be, the fact is that biologically based inequalities are not as important as socially created inequalities. It seems to us that in Chandigarh as in many other parts of the country, it is largely the socially created inequalities which provide the major basis for the system of social stratification.

We may mention here that the human family, in one form or another, has existed since the dawn of history, and there is little sign of its disappearance. It still constitutes the most primary group in society. It consists of a group of people in a face-to-face relationship, linked together by reason of their common interests and abode. As a family is formed for certain specific purposes, it also constitutes an organisation to achieve these purposes. But the central purpose of the family is the propagation and rearing of children. Every society, therefore, has some kind of regulation of sexual behaviour which is considered necessary for stability and continuity of the family. Actually, the form of the family has changed enormously in the course of history, from the time when tribal loyalities were paramount and the family could satisfy all human needs to the present time when it is a unit of limited size for diminished functions. The fact is that the family had varied a great deal over the time and across cultural barriers. Actually, the family also changes in the course of a person's own experience. Before any children are born, there is the nuptual stage when the couple try to get to know one another and define their new position in society. With the arrival of children, the child rearing stage begins and this has the effect of converting the family into a more definite social unit. From now onwards, the roles of the marriage partners change from being simply those of husband and wife to being also those of mother and father. Thus regardless of the cultural setting, the family is basically characterised by three features: first, a mating relationship; second, some kind of shared economic provision for children and, third, a common dwelling or home. What needs to be emphasized is that differential functioning of any of these features can affect the bringing up of children, their survival and also their adaptation to the culture of their society. The process whereby children are taught about proper ways of behaving, particularly within the family is called socialization. And it involves learning all manners of things. Manners and modes of acting which are learnt very early in life become habits which are extremely tenacious and persistent. The significance of the family, therefore, extends throughout life. But at times of illness, the effects of the family become specially significant. For example, the kind of care a child can hope to get in a joint family may be vastly different from what he may get in a nuclear family. This has been brought out in a study done in four villages of Haryana. The findings revealed that help-seeking pattern in the case of childhood illnesses was qualitatively better in a joint family than in a nuclear family.[4] Similar findings have emerged from certain other studies. Erosion of the joint family which one witnesses today in Chandigarh, therefore, has its own adverse effects on the bringing up of children. And this problem gets accentuated, particularly in the scheduled caste families where mothers are forced to work outside their homes for supplementing family income. Thus, there is a linkage between a child's biological environment, family environment and physical environment. How the interaction of these three environments affects a child's health status needs to be looked into carefully. From the environmental viewpoint, the health status of an individual is determined by the interplay and balanced intergration of two ecological universes—the internal environment, and the external environment, which surrounds them. The external environment consists of three major interlinked components—physical, social and biological. The physical environment encompasses the non-living things and physical forces affecting them e.g. water, air, ventilation lighting, noise, and climate. The biological environment includes the living things of the plant and animal kingdom. On the other hand, social environment comprises of a complex interplay of factors and conditions such as values, traditions, customs, beliefs and attitudes.

Health status of children, therefore, can be viewed properly only in relation to their environment. For instance, much of the child wastage in Chandigarh's urban and rural areas can be attributed to environmental deprivation of one or the other kind. During 1988, in Chandigarh, 319 still births were recorded out of a total of 17,266 births. The environment in the villages and urban slums where we undertook a micro-level study of the ICDS programme was deficient because of the unhygenic conditions. Much of malnutrition among children there and also the high levels of infections can be attributed to defects in their physical, biological and social environment. Children there remained exposed to a host of infectious diseases. The absence of adequate facilities for disposal of excreta accounted for the high prevalence of bacterial, viral, protozol and helmenthic diseases. We noted that a substantial number of children there were living in conditions of poverty and insanitation. They lived in substandard dwellings, lacking in space, cleanliness, ventilation and sunlight. Such conditions tended to increase the incidence of various diseases, particularly, airborne diseases[7]. Over-crowding was one of the factors responsible for children contacting such diseases at an early age. But then the kinship system is such that it brings the child into regular contact with many other children at a very young age thus increasing its exposure to disease. We hardly need to stress that among children whose immune response is not yet developed, the risk of catching multiple infections is always high. But what needs to be highlighted is that the synergism between malnutrition and infections leads to devastating effects on health. We may mention here that compared with their health status, the health status of children residing in privileged areas of the city was far better. This was because they enjoyed better incomes, better living conditions, better school enrolment ratios, better environmental and and personal health services.

The pattern of mortality, including the pattern of infant and child mortality, in Chandigarh reflects the preponderance of environment-related diseases, both air-borne and water-borne. We have observed in a village of Chandigarh that maximum neglect of female children took place in families where the mothers were working outside their homes for long hours and where there were no elderly relatives to take care of them. This is not to say that other factors have no influence on the neglect of female children. A recent study, done in two villages of Chandigarh, has brought to light the fact that in families having preponderance of female children, the neglect of the female child started right from the time of disposal of placenta. While the placenta of a male child was disposed of in a socially prescribed ritualistic manner, such care was not taken in the case of a female child[8].

Only a few research studies on childhood mortality, done in this region, can boast of attaining a reasonable level of methodological sophistication. The findings of such studies deserve special attention. For example, during the three years of Khanna Study, the death rate from acute diarrhoeal disease, pneumonia, typhoid, fever, and measles ranged from 187 to 80 per 100,000 of the general population. Tetanus alone accounted for nearly one-third of all deaths among the newborn. This was attributed to insanitary methods of cutting the umbilical stump at child birth[9]. During 1987-88, out of 579 cases of tetanus, as many as 187 deaths took place in the country thus showing that conditions preciptitating tetanus still exist[10]. A study done in PGI, Chandigarh, has revealed that in most of the 44 cases of tetanus admitted for treatment, deliveries were conducted by untrained midwives[11]. Our own study of the role of 42 'dais' in Haryana has revealed that most of them were untrained[12]. The available statistics in Chandigarh have shown that in rural areas, domiciliary treatment at the time of birth was provided by 'untrained midwives' in hundred percent of the cases[13]. The Khanna study in rural

Punjab had brought out that of the total deaths in the age group 1-5, 70 percent of deaths occurred in the second year of life, 19.2 percent in the third year, 7.5 percent in the fourth year and 3.3 percent in the fifth year[14]. In 1986, out of a total of 4501 deaths that took place in Chandigarh, as many as 830 deaths were of infants (18.04% under one year of age and 25.26% under 14 years). And, of the total deaths registered, about 39.10 percent of deaths were of females. Generally speaking, if one were to draw the mortality curve by age in Chandigarh then one would readily see that it has a U-Shape : high in the first years of life, declining rapidly in the second and third years until age ten ; remaining low until middle age then increasing at a rapid rate during older years[15]. The major difference between male and female mortality continues to occur at the weaning period i.e. 6-24 months of age. And malnutrition is still more pronounced among female children than among male children. We may mention here that the Khanna study had recorded 74 deaths per 1000 population for females, compared to 50 per thousond among males, taking the first five years as a whole[16]. The gap between male and female mortality was found to be greatest at the reproductive ages. This was largely attributable to high fertility, which increased the possibilty of maternal care. Normally, repeated pregnancies followed by prolonged lactation periods will, apart from other things, produce sustained needs for high quality protein in the diet. When these needs are not met, particularly in the case of women residing in underprivileged areas,—'maternal depletion syndrome' may occur. This may ultimately result in premature aging and early deaths among females.

What needs to be recognised is that social and economic conditions greatly influence patterns of morbidity and mortality and the environmental factors play an important role in the occurrence and spread of diseases among children. The environment in which children live determines their exposure and susceptibility to diseases.

In Chandigarh, the scheduled caste people, who make up 14.09 percent of the population, have traditionally formed a distinctive social stratum at the base of stratification system[17]. The majority of them, including children, have occupied the most subservient occupational statuses, being employed as labourers and as unskilled and semi-skilled manual workers in industries. In their work places, children often breathe in air laden with soot, partially burnt particles of metals, rubber and asbestos and gasses of many kinds including sulphur dioxide and carbon monoxide. In some of the worst affected areas of Chandigarh, one could identify thousands of foreign particles in the polluted atmosphere. The burning of fuels, the emission of vehicular smoke and fumes, consequent of a large number of four-wheelers and two-wheelers in the city, have also led to the problem of atmospheric pollution to which children are exposed. Even plants and crops have been adversely affected by atmospheric pollution. As a result of this, animals and birds too suffer from lung conditions, like anthracosis. It needs to be emphasised that ozonides are formed in places where there is high petrol consumption. These gases can cause considerable irritation and harm to animal and human mucus membrane.

It may also be pointed out that Chandigarh's industrial complex is located in the south-eastern part of the city. The major industries include a paper board mill, two nickle plating industries, a flour mill, a milk plant and a drug manufacturing unit. In addition, there are 1,696 small scale units. The effluents of these industries are also channelized into a common sewer which is connected with the main sewer that carries the entire Chandigarh sewage to the treatment plant. These industries have contributed considerably to the problem of environmental pollution which affects the health of women and children. On the other hand, in the villages of Chandigarh, within the home environment, the discomfort and harm caused by burning leaves, buffalo dung cakes and smoke-emitting fuels were a serious hazard to the inmates, particularly, women and children. Lack of proper planning and legislation and its enforcement are partly responsible for environmental problems which play havoc with the lives of women and children in the under-privileged areas. The lack of safe and sufficient drinking water supply in Chandigarh's urban slums and villages further complicates the problem of poor sanitary conditions. Besides, over-crowding and lack of ventilation also increases the chances of catching a host of air-borne infections.

In Chandigarh, health care services are being provided through a network of one primary health centre, 12 sub-centres and 24 despensaries, including 2 Ayurvedic and 3 Homeopathic dispensaries. A recent survey has revealed a fairly high level of coverage of immunization (80 percent of children were fully immunized and 15.2 percent were partially immunized). Also, a total of 21422 children (5-15 years) were inoculated against typhoid[18]. In addition, about 8,000 packets of oral rehydration salt (ORT) were being supplied every year through subcentres and dispensaries. All this would provide enough evidence of the sincerity of purpose on the part of the administration and all those who are, directly or indirectly, involved in the planning, organization and execution of intervention programmes, meant for women and children. Family Planning Services in Chandiargh are an essential component of the health care system. The primary responsibility for the delivery of health services rests wlth the administration. The family welfare programme is centrally sponsored. The responsibility for the formulation of an overall policy for the programme, therefore, lies with the Central Government. The present policy is to promote family planning on the basis of voluntary and informed acceptance with full community participation. Tne family welfare programme in Chandigarh, therefore, lays emphasis on a 'two-child family'. Greater emphasis is now being laid on spacing methods along with the terminal methods. The main thrust of the programme is to take the services to the people and motivate families to adopt the small family norm. During 1988-89, a total of 2926 sterlizations were performed (83.6 percent of the target was achieved)[19]. The couple protection rate was quite high as compared to national figures. The total fertility rate of 2.7 was significantly lesser than the all India level (3.6). The fertility rate was higher in the age group 25-29, followed by age group 20-24, and age group 30-34, respectively. Eligible couples were also protected through temporary methods of family planning. Reportedly, more than 60 percent of the target was achieved.

A WHO-sponsored study in the Union Territory of Chandigarh brought out that the acceptance and continuation rate of family planning methods could be increased considerably if the free-choice approach was adopted[20]. Another study has also shown that the continuation rate of oral contraceptives could be increased if more stress was laid on adequate follow-up and counselling. In Chandigarh, in addition to family planning services, MCH services are also provided at the various dispensaries and sub-centres. During 1980-89, tetanus toxoid was provided to 13,343 pregnant women. Yet there were many gaps in the implementation of these programmes as coverage of immunization and provision of health and other welfare services was much lower in the underprivileged areas including the urban slums[21].

Though the growth of population is taking place all over the country, it has different significance or repercussions in different places, including Chandigarh. And it also has different repercussions on the health and nutritional status of women and children. The population in Chandigarh is likely to rise sharply in the years ahead as more young adults swell the ranks of potential parents and improved medical care advances the life expectancy. The planners and other interventionalists in Chandigarh, therefore, have to assess how this trend would affect the hopes and aspirations of women and children for higher living standards, better education, and greater health facilities. They may have to reexamine the three key resources – food, space and jobs, to grapple with the problem of over-population. What needs to be emphasised is that the deficit in any one of these depends as much on the life styles, technological capabilities, patterns of production and consumption as on population density.

A number of nutrition intervention programmes have been started in Chandigarh. A combination of approaches have been adopted like supplementary feeding, nutrition education, fortification and enrichment of foods and extending the existing food supplies. Under the ICDS scheme, a package of services relating to health, nutrition and educational needs of children below six years of age is being provided. Two ICDS projects have been functioning in Chandigarh. These projects cover a population of 1,97,627 (54.6% males and 45.4% females). There is litttle difference in regard to sex-wise coverage in these two projects. (Appendix I) Of the 36,613 children being covered, 3,524 were below 6 months, 4,455 between the ages 6 months to one year, 9,847 between one year to three years, and, 18,787 between three years to six years. (Appendix II). Of the 3152 children, between 6 months to 3 years, who were eligible for ICDS services, only (37.4%) were receiving supplementary nutrition. In contrast, only 39 percent of the children, between 3 and 6 years, were receiving supplementary nutrition (Appendix III). However, of the 2967 pregnant women identified, as many as 1706 (60.5%) were receiving supplementary nutrition. At the same time, of the 3242 lactating mothers identified, 1796 (55.4%) were receiving supplementary nutrition. (Appendix IV).

An assessment of the nutritional status of children was done on the basis of weight for age measurement at the anganwadis.

Thus, of the 1646 children between the ages one and three years, 787 were found to be 'normal', 541 in Grade I and 297 in Grade II. Only 19 children were found to be in Grade III and 2 in Grade IV. Of 6025 children, in the age group 3 to 6 years, 2704 were found to be 'normal', 2242 in Grade I, 1062 in Grade II and 17 in Grade III (Appendix V) All malnourished children were supposed to be on 'double diet'. However, only 21 children, between 6 months and 3 years, and, 17 children between 3 years and 6 years, were receiving 'double ration' as provided at their respective anganwadis.

The interest and wellbeing of children is the main concern of every society that is committed to the philosophy of social welfare. The Constitution of India states that there will be no discrimination on the grounds of sex, religion and race between citizens of India, and that nothing shall prevent the State from making any special provision for women and children. It is further laid down in the Directive Principles of State Policy that, "The State shall, in particular, direct its policy towards securing the health and strength of workers, men and women so that the tender aged children are not abused and that citizens are not forced by economic necessity to enter avocations, unsuited to their age or strength". It is also provided that "State shall endeavour to provide, within a period of ten years from the commencement of this Constitution, for free and compulsory education for all children until they complete the age of fourteen years. The Constitution mandate has been followed up in a number of enactments, to safeguard the interest of children, particularly those from weaker sections of society.

It is in this spirit of the Indian Constitution that the planners in Chandigarh have tried to bring infant mortality under control through a reinforced maternal and child health care orientation. This can certainly provide some ground for the small family norm. But the emphasis on infants' survival does not ensure continued improvement of the health status of children representing weaker sections for the simple reason that the environment in which they live continues to be deficient in one way or the other. Thus if the lot of children has to be improved in a speedy manner, one has to give careful attention to the interrelationship between health, nutrition, physical environment, education, gender and power inequalities, and access to health, family welfare and nutritional care.

REFFRENCES

1. Premi, M.K. (1991) India's Population. An Analysis of 1991 census provisional results B.R. Publishing Corporation, Delhi.
2. Census of Government Employees, Chandigarh Administration (1987) Statistical Cell, Finance. Department, Chandigarh.
3. Kakar, D.N. (1977) Folk and Modern Medicine—A North Indian Case Study, New Asian Publishers, New Delhi.
4. Chopra Suksham (1984) People's Perception about Childhood illnesses and their Therapeutic Practices and preferences in four selected villages of Raipur Rani Block, Ph.D. thesis (Unpublished) PGI, Chandigarh.
5. Kakar, D.N. (1988) Primary Health Care and Traditional Medical Practitioners. Sterling Publishers, New Delhi.
6. Dunnel, K. and Wright (1972) Medicine Takers, Prescribes and Hoarders. Routledge and Kagan Paul, London.

7. Kakar, D.N. Chopra, S. (1990) Environmental Factors Affecting Health in an Urban Slum. In: The New Environmental Age (Eds. Sapru, R.K; and Shyama Bhardwaj) Ashish Publishing House, New Delhi.

8. Kakar, D.N., et al (1990) Beliefs and Practices Related to disposal of Human Placenta. The Nursing Journal of India, Vol. XXX No. 12.

9. Wyon, B. and Gordon, J. (1971) The Khanna Study. Population Problems in the Rural Punjab. Harvard University Press.

10. Health Information India (1988) Government of India, Ministry of Health and Family Welfare, New Delhi.

11. Bhakoo, O.N., Garg, S.K. (1976) Socioeconomic, Epidemiological Study of Neonatal Tetanus. Indian Paediatrics, Vol. 13, pp 545-552.

12. Kakar, D.N. (1980) Dais—The Traditional Birth Attendants in Village India, New Asian Publishers, Delhi.

13. Registration of Births and Deaths Act 1969. Annual Report (1986) Union Territory of Chandigarh.

14. Wyon, B. and Gordon J. (1971) op. cit.

15. Health Statistics (1990). Directorate of Health Services, U.T., Chandigarh.

16. Census Government Employees Chandigarh Administration (1987) Statistical Cell. Finance Department, Chandigarh.

17. Directorate of Census Operations (1990) U.T. Admins-tration, Chandigarh.

18. Directorate of Family Welfare (1989-90) U.T., Adminis-tration, Chandigarh.

19. Directorate of Census operation (1990), U.T., Adminis-tration, Chandigarh.

20. Kakar, D.N. (1984) Women and Family Planning. Sterling Publishers, New Delhi.

21. Kakar, D.N., et al (1990) Report on Situational Anlysis of women and children in Chandigarh. (Report Sub-mitted to UNICEF, Chandigarh).

3

ICDS : A Macro-level Survey

In the National Policy for Children, the nation's children are rightly considered as a supremely important assest. The nation, no doubt, is responsible for their nurture and solicitude. The Poiicy clearly states, "Children's programmes should find a prominent part in our national plans for the development of human resources".[1] The aim is to provide equal opportunities for development to all children during the period of growth. The policy of the State is to provide adequate services to children, both before and after birth and through the period of growth, to ensure their full physical, social and mental development. And it is made explicitly clear that the State shall progressively increase the scope of such services so that, within a reasonable time, all children in the country enjoy optimum conditions for their balanced growth. It has been proposed therefore to adopt several measures towards the attainment of laid down objectives. Of the plethora of proposed measures to be adopted, the following deserve special attention form the consideration of the ICDS :

(1) All children shall be covered by a comprehensive health programme;

(2) Programmes shall be implemented to provide nutrition services with the object of removing deficiencies in the diet of children;

(3) Progrmmes will be undertaken for the general improvement of the health and for the care, nutrition and nutrition education of expectant and nursing mothers;

(4) To ensure equality of opportunity, special assistance shall be provided to all children belonging to the weaker sections of the society, such as children belonging to the Scheduled Castes and Scheduled Tribes; and

(5) In organising services for children, efforts would be directed to strengthen family ties so that full potentialities of growth of children are realised within the normal family, neighbourhood and community environment.

Again, it is clearly brought out in the National Policy for Children that for formulating programmes in different sectors, priority shall be given to the programmes relating to—

(a) preventive and promotive aspects of child health;

(b) nutrition for infants and children in the pre-school age along with nutrition for nursing and expectant mothers;

(c) maintenance, education and training of orphan and destitute children;

(d) cretches and other facilities for the care of children of working and ailing mothers; and

(e) care, education, training and rehabilitation of handicapped children.[2]

Keeping in view these priorities, considerable progress has

been made in the provision of services for children during the last two decades. Provision of Integrated Child Development Services (ICDS), therefore, is in conformity with the National Policy for Children. The ICDS scheme is being considered as a preventive and developmental effort. The most significant aspect of this scheme is that it extends beyond the existing health and education systems to reach children and their mothers residing in villages and urban slums. And as mentioned earlier, it provides a package of services comprising :

(i) non-formal pre-school educatton.

(ii) immunisation.

(iii) health check-up.

(iv) supplementary nutrition.

(v) medical services.

(vi) nutrition and health education for women.

The ICDS scheme, it seems, is likely to be extended to every community development block. The idea is to reach the poorest of the poor in all underprivileged areas of the country especially villages and urban slums. The increasing stress on the implementation of the ICDS scheme is indicative of the Government of India's commitment to child development as a policy priority. It is from this consideration that the impact of the ICDS programme is assessed periodically by experts representing different specialities. Annual surveys are carried out throughout the country, following guidelines and instructions laid down by the Bio-Statistics division of the Central Technical Committee, (on Health and Nutrition), of the All India Institute of Medical Sciences[3]. The Central Technical Committee has, from time to time, sought the cooperation of faculty members of various medical colleges and institutes for their help in carrying out annual surveys to assess the impact of the ICDS programme in their respective areas. The findings presented here pertain to a survey of the ICDS programme, carried out in 1991, in six selected anganwadis of the Union Territory of Chandigarh. The data for this survey were gathered by a team of doctors and social science personnel of the Department of Community Medicine of the PGI under the overall supervision of the author in the capacity of a consultant. We may just mention here that before the collection of data, all members of the team were clearly explained the objectives of the macro-level survey. Carrying out this survey was a time-bound activity, and we may as well mention that all members of the team participated in it rather enthusiastically. The selection of the six anganwadis for this survey was done, in accordance with the laid down criteria. Information about coverage of the ICDS projects I and II in Chandigarh is given in the Appendeces (1 to 5).

Based on this survey, a brief report was prepared for the Central Technical Committee, in Delhi, for inclusion in their 'national report'[4]. A write up on some aspects of the ICDS programme in Chandigarh had also appeared in the 'Community Medicine Newsletter' of the PGI (1991).[5] Only certain selected findings of this survey are discussed here with a view to highlighting some important aspects of the ICDS scheme in Chandigarh. To begin with, we may state that of the six anganwadis, surveyed in Chandigarh, only two were found to be functioning in proper buildings. Yet all the six anganwadis were well-attended (on, an average, 40 children attended an aganwadi). These six anganwadis were supposed to serve 1052 households in their respective areas. For the purpose of this survey, only 983 (93.4%) households were contacted as the occupants of other households were not available at the time of the survey. Caste-wise, 38.9 percent of the heads of households belonged to the scheduled castes; 37.5% to the higher castes; 19.9 percent to the backward classes and the remaining 3.7%

to the minorities. But, occupation-wise, the majority of them were found to be engaged in service (61.8%), while 15.4 percent were businessmen, 8.7 percent were cultivators and 6.5 percent were either retired personnel or unemployed. (Table 1)

TABLE 1

Characteristics of the Respondents Surveyed in Six Selected Anganwadis in Chandigarh.

Characteristics	Number	Percentage
Caste Status		
Higher Castes	382	37.5
Scheduled Caste	196	38.9
Backward Classes	368	19.9
Minorities	37	3.7
Occupational Status		
(i) Service	607	61.8
(ii) Business	151	15.4
(iii) Artisans	87	8.8
(iv) Retired/unemployed	63	6.4
(v) Labourers and others	32	3.3
(vi) Small Traders	43	4.3

Total Number of Respondents=983

However, age-wise, only 14.9% of the members of the surveyed households were below 6 years of age. Of the rest, 25.9% were in the age group 15-45 years. Only 12.7% of them were above 45 years of age. (Table 2)

TABLE 2

Age-wise Distribution of Population Covered by the Six Selected Anganwadis in Chandigarh

Age Group (in years)	Number	Percentage
0-1	124	2.4
1-2	117	2.2
2-3	137	2.9
3-6	368	7.2
6-15	1303	25.8
15.45	2358	46.8
45 and above	630	12.7
Total	5037	100.0

During this survey, we were able to identify as many as 41 pregnant women and 117 lactating mothers. The majority of them either belonged to the scheduled castes (52.2%) or the backward classes (28.2%). Again, the majority of them were either in the age-group 16-25 years (43.5%) or in the age-group 25-35 years (46.1%). It was heartening to note that more than three-fourths of them had received tetanus toxide. We also learnt that over three-fourths of them (76.9%) had received ante-natal care, right from the second month of pregnancy onwards, 29.1 percent had received it one-to-two times, and 47.8 percent thrce or more times. The providers of ante-natal care included : medical officers (39.4%) ANMS and LHVs (27.4%) (Table 3). But then we found that the utilization of nutritional supplementary services was much less, both during pregnancy (35.8%) and during lactational period (29.9%). At the same time, we found slightly better coverage in regard to the distribution of iron and folic acid tablets to lactating mothers (41.1%). We also found that the assistance at the time of delivery was obtained by all these lactating mothers. The majority of them had delivered the child, either in their own homes (48.7) or in the general hospital (41.1%) and the remaining (10.3%) had gone to the private nursing homes or clinics for this purpose. It was noted that only 14.6 percent of them had started giving first feed to the child, six hours aftfer birth. Another 48.6 percent had delayed the feed for more than 48 hours. Postnatal care was also received by a majority of them (69.2%). And the providers of postnatal care included, trained dais, ANMs and LHVs. As many as 76.1 percent of these lactating women were not using any fertility regulating methods at the time of this survey. (Table 4) However, of those who were using family planning methods, 11 were using conventional contraceptives; 4 Cu.T.; and 2 oral pills, Sterilization was adopted by only 3 of them. Of the households surveyed, as many as 457 households were found to be eligible for the ICDS. And of these, only 250 households, (54.7%) were actually utilising the ICDS. And in these households, only 17.9 percent of the children, in 12-24 months age-group, were attending the aganwadis (Table 5).

TABLE 3

Characteristics of the Lactating Mothers Covered by the Six Selected Anganwadis in Chandigarh

Characteristics	Number	Percentage
(i) *Caste Status*		
Higher	53	15.3
Scheduled	60	52.2
Backward	18	28.2
Others	5	4.3
(ii) *Antenatal Care*		
Yes	90	76.9
No	24	20.5
Not recorded	3	2.6
(iii) *Number of times antenatal care received*		
1-2	34	29.1
3-4	33	28.2
5-6	11	9.4
6 & more	12	10.2
Not received/Not recorded	27	23.1
(iv) *Type of Personnel who attended delivery*		
Medical officers	46	39.4
Dai	7	5.7
ANM/LHV	32	27.4
Others (RMPs)	5	4.3
Not recorded/	27	23.2

(v) *Immunization Status (Complete dose)*		
Yes	92	78.6
No	16	13.7
Not Recorded/	9	7.7

Total Number of Respondents=117

TABLE 4

Distribution of Lactating Mothers according to their Initiation of First Breast feed and the Use of Fertility Regulating Methods in six selected Anganwadis in Chandigarh.

Breast feed/use of Initiation of FRM	Number	Percentage
(i) *Breast feed*		
Within 6 hours	17	14.6
6 to 24 hours	36	30.7
24-48 hours	21	17.9
48 hours & above	32	27.4
Not recorded	11	9.3
(ii) *Use of Fertility Regulating Methods*		
Yes	20	17.1
No	89	76.1
Not recorded	8	6.8

Total Number of Respondents=117

TABLE 5

Caste-wise Distribution of Respondents according to their Use of ICDS services in six Selected Anganwadi, in Chandigarh

Caste Status	Use of ICDS Services Yes	No	Total
Higher castes	81 (45.2)	98 (54.8)	179 100.0
Scheduled castes	130 (59.9)	87 (39.1)	217 (100.0)
Lower and backward Classes	39 (54.9)	32 (45.1)	71 100.0
Total	250 (54.7)	207 (45.3)	457 (100.0)

Significantly, 86.3 percent of the children, in these households, had received the BCG. Complete immunization doses were received by 78.68 percent of the children. In addition, 52.1 percent of the children had received measles vaccine. There was relatively less malnutrition among the children who were covered under the ICDS scheme. However, only 7.6 percent of the children had received Vitamin A and 8.1 percent had received Iron and folic acid. The distribution of Vitamin A and Iron folic acid tablets was inadequate in all age-groups. We learnt during, the survey, that the stress laid on non-formal education was far from adequate. Also, there was a general lack of awareness among the parents about the provision of Vitamin A and Iron and folic acid tablets for their children. They had no idea about the benefit of these supplements to their children. The reasons for non-utilization of the ICDS were : children going to a private school; lack of variety in food served at the anganwadi; lack of proper care; lack of educational facilities; and, lack of interest. Obviously, there was little or no community participation in the ICDS programme. The survey team was of the view that this aspect should be given the top priority by the higher authorities. The anganwadi workers had little contact with the pregnant women of their respective areas. They did not know how to increase their participation in the ICDS programme. To be more precise, they needed help in the planning of efficient and effective health and nutrition education for the pregnant women.

It may be pointed out here that there are hardly any methodologically sound studies on the long-term impact of the ICDS. The few studies that have been carried out are briefly discussed here. In one of these studies, it was found that the coverage of antenatal services to pregnant women was almost double in the ICDS group (71.9%) as compared to the non-ICDS or control group (40.3%). The utilization of trained medical personnel, for conducting home deliveries, too was found to be significantly higher in the ICDS group (76.3%) than in the non-ICDS group (49.4%). However, preference for home deliveries was uniformly favoured by both these groups. Similarly, utilization of post-natal services by the lactating mothers was found to be relatively higher in the ICDS group than in the non-ICDS group. However, the overall success rate of coverage was less than 50 percent in rural areas and 30 to 40 percent in tribal areas.[6] In another study, it was brought out that the immunization coverage in some areas had doubled or trebled, after the introduction of the ICDS.[7] Yet another evaluation, carried out in 70 ICDS centres, located in urban areas of Madras, has revealed that the coverage of poliomyelitis was 16.4 percent (complete 3 doses) in non-ICDS areas as compared to 42.7 percent in the ICDS areas after a period of two years or more.[8] Similarly, there was another study, in which it was shown that the immunization coverage of 3 vaccines for children, reached as high a level as 50 percent compared to the ICDS baseline data, where it was only 21 percent. A five-fold increase in Tetanus Toxide immunization for Pregnant mothers was also reported.[9] These findings of different studies are indicative of the fact that the ICDS is an efficient avenue for the extension of immunization coverage and prevention of disabilities. Thus, one could feed on the hope that with greater coordination between the ICDS and the health department functionaries, complete targets of immunization could be met by the year 2000 AD.

As regard the impact of nutritional supplements, a survey conducted in 15 projects, out of a total of 33 original projects, showed considerable reduction in the incidence of severe malnutrition among children 0-6 years, (from 21.9% to 5.4%). Similarly, there was some reduction in the incidence of moderate malnutrition among children 0-6 years (from 23.3 to 17.2 percent). But there was a dramatic reduction in the case of severely malnoursished children below three years of age (from 29.2% to 6%)[10]. Another longitudinal study had also shown that there was reduction in the cases of severe malnutrition amongst the preschool children, from 19.1% to 6.3% as compared with reduction in the cases of moderate malnutrition (from 27.0% to 19.7%)[11]. In yet another study, the incidence of moderate and severe malnutrition among children was found to be 3.5 percent in the ICDS projects as compared to 38.5 percent in the non-ICDS projects (matched control group).[12] In one specific study, the management of severe malnutrition, at the anganwadi had shown a reduction in mortality and morbidity rates. (The mortality rate at the anganwadi was found to be 3.8% to 5.8% in rural areas as compared to 15% to 35% in the hospital population). Another comparative study, carried out in the ICDS and non-ICDS population, has shown a higher infant mortality rate in the non-ICDS group as compared to the ICDS group (rural 85.5% vs. 67.0%; urban, 87.0% vs. 80.0%). But the infant mortality rate was found to be higher among the males as compared to the females both in the ICDS and the non-ICDS groups[14]. In yet another important study, carried out in an ICDS area by the All India Institute of Medical Sciences, 4,292 children suffering from severe malnutrition, were followed up, for a period of 6 to 12 weeks. This study revealed that there was improvement in 85 percent of the cases, no change, in 6.3 percent of the cases and deterioration in 3.6% of the cases. Only 3 percent of the children had died.[15] These findings were considered encouraging enough to extend the ICDS scheme to other areas. It has also been brought out that "Special Research Data", reveal that neonatal mortality rate, in rural and tribal ICDS groups, was much lower (51.2%) as compared to SRS figures (72.9%). States-wise however, neonatal mortality rates varied considerably in the ICDS groups from 18.0 percent in Kerala to 72.7% in Uttar Pradesh.[16]

As mentioned earlier, one of the functions of the anganwadi worker is to impart health and nutrition education to pregnant women and lactating mothers with a view to enhancing their capability to look after their children. In an evaluative study, conducted in two states of India, it was brought out that nearly one-third of the mothers who were given health and nutrition education stated that their "children have learned good habits, numbers and poetry at the anganwadi". It was also brought out that while 64 percent of them 'had the knowledge of ORS', only 52 percent knew how to prepare it at home.[17]

All these studies are full of optimism. But we know that the true test of the pudding lies in its eating. Therefore we may mention here that the World Summit for Children, on September 30, 1990, had adopted certain well-defined goals to be attained by the year 2000. It might be a good idea to see, how many of the following 12 selected goals are actually attained by India by the year 1995, that is, 20 years after the ICDS scheme had been in operation :

(i) A reduction in the incidence of low birth weight (2.5 kg or less) to less than 10 percent.

(ii) A one-third reduction in iron deficiency anaemia among women.

(iii) A one-third reduction in under-five death rates (or a reduction to below 70 per 1,000 live births—whichever is less.

(iv) A halving of maternal mortality rate.

(v) Achievement and maintenance of at least 85% immunization coverage of one-year-old children and universal tetanus immunization for women of the child-bearing years.

(vi) A halving of child deaths caused by diarrhoea and a 25% reduction in the incidence of diarrhoeal diseases.

(vii) All women to have access to pre-natal care, a trained attendant during child birth and referred for high-risk pregnancies and obstetric emergencies.

(viii) Growth monitoring and promotion to be institutionalised.

(ix) A 90% reduction in measles cases and a 95% reduction in measles deaths, compared to pre-immunization levels.

(x) The eradication of polio.

(xi) The elimination of neonatal tetanus.

(xii) A one-third reduction in child deaths caused by acute respiratory infections.[18]

It would also be useful to assess as to what extent beneficiaries in an anganwadi area were using some form of oral rehydration.

By way of reference, we may point out that in 1971, some form of oral rehydration therapy was used by one in three famiiies, in the developing world. Thus one million lives were being saved each year[19]. Similarly, in order to assess the impact of health and nutrition education component of the ICDS programme, it would be useful to record how many parents of the beneficiaries know that continued feeding of a child at risk, and an extra meal a day, in the week or so after the illness, is essential to protect normal growth. Future studies should include specific indicators to assess the true impact of the ICDS. It would be exceedingly interesting to determine whether parents know that the diarrhoeal disease can be prevented by breast feeding, by using latrines, by keeping food and water clean, and by washing hands before touching food. Only when this type of information starts percolating to the parents, can one say that the efforts of national and international organizations like the UNICEF and WHO have started bearing fruit.

REFERENCES

1. The Rights of tne Child (1990) Report of the World Summit for Children. Indian University Association for Continuing Education, Indraprastha Estate, New Delhi.

2. The Rights of the Child (1990) Ibid.

3. Integrated Child Development Services. Annual Survey (1990-91). General Guidelines and Instructions for Data Collection, and Tabulation Analysis. Biostatistics Division of Central Cell. Central Technical Committee on Health and Nutrition (Cyclostyled), AIIMS, New Delhi.

4. Kakar, D.N. (1991) Action Oriented Report—Annual Survey (1990-91). A Brief Report submitted to Central Technical Committee on Health and Nutrition. All India Institute of Medical Sciences, New Delhi.

5. Kakar, D.N. (1991) Community Medicine, Newsletter, Vol. I No. I Department of Community Medicine, PGI, Chandigarh.

6. Integrated Child Development Services (1990) Central Technical Committee, Department of Gastroenterology and Human Nutrition. All India Institute of Medical Sciences, New Delhi.

7. Jayam, S. (1983) Disability Prevention in ICDS, Paper Presented at the ICDS Annual Convention, New Delhi.

8. ICDS—Integrated Child Development Services in India (1984) UNICEF, New Delhi.

9. Integrated Child Development Services (1990) Central Technical Committee. op. cit.

10. Management of Severely Malnourished Children by village workers in ICDS in India (1983). All India Institute of Medical Sciences, New Delhi.

11. Integrated Child Development Services (1990) Central Technical Committee. P. 13 op. cit.

12. Integrated Child Development Services (1990) Ibid.

13. Integrated Child Development Services (1984) UNICEF, New Delhi.

14. Integrated Child Development Services (1990) Ibid.

15. Bhatnagar, S. et al (1982) Effect of Food Supplementation in the last trimester of Pregnancy and early postnatal period on maternal weight and infant growth. All India Institute of Medical Sciences, New Delhi.

16. Integrated Child Development Services (1990) op. cit.

17. Integrated Child Development Services (1990) op. cit.

18. The Rights of the Child (1990) World Summit for Children.

19. The State of World's Children (1991) Published for United Nations Children's Fund (UNICEF, Oxford University Press.

4

ICDS : A Micro-level Study

There can be little doubt that the health of children, our greatest national resource, is vital to our country's future. Yet we do not seem to be taking this matter seriously. No doubt, we have started the ICDS scheme, which, by all accounts, is of great value to the children. But then we often feel shy of taking stock of the true situation of the anganwadis, of facing the reality. The findings, presented in this chapter, may acquaint the readers with the true situation of the anganwadis in Chandigarh's villages and urban slums.

The Micro-level study was undertaken with the sole purpose of understanding the functioning of the ICDS scheme from a holistic viewpoint. The study was sponsored by the Postgraduate Institute of Medical Education and Research, Chandigarh.

METHODOLOGY

We have laid stress here both on qualitative and quantitative aspects. The meanigful questions which one may like to discuss in connection with any subject matter are of two kinds:

verbal problems, whose solution depends on determining the use of words, and factual problems, whose solution depends on the determination of some question or fact. It has been characteristic of the scientific as opposed to the philosophical tradition in the social sciences that has led to a certain dislike of discussion of verbal problems. No one would deny that the directing of attention to thc facts of the social sciences rather than to ways of talking about them is desirable. But at the same time, words are the tools of all science, and a certain amount of attention must be given to tools, although such attention to tools should be regarded as a means, and not as an end, of social investigation. The objectives of our study were : (i) to identify factors affecting implementation of the ICDS scheme in Chandigarh ; (ii) to recommend ways and means of overcoming these factors ; (iii) to suggest additional social indicators for incorporation in the overall evaluation strategy ; and (iv) to evolve strategies for seeking community participation. The study focussed on 20 anganwadis, selected on a random basis, from Chandigarh's villages and urban slums. Efforts were made subsequently to find out the extent to which some of the findings of this study were similar to those emerging from a rapid survey of 80 additional anganwadis, selected on a random basis. This subsequent input was meant to understand the magnitude of the problems identified earlier. The idea was to draw a picture which reflected the true reality of the ICDS scheme in our study area. The data were collected by persons trained in behavioural sciences.

The methodological tools used for the collection of data included a semi-structured interview schedule and the interview guidelines. Data were also collected through participant observation. Besides, the case study material was collected to understand the motives of the anganwadi workers in joining the ICDS scheme. The study was started in April 1971, and completed by March, 1992. The findings are discussed under topical headings.

The Physical Environment of Anganwadis

Of the 100 anganwadis, included in the study, 58 anganwadis were found to be functioning for over a decade, 31 for 8 to 10 years, and the remaining eleven for 6 to 7 years. (Table 6).

TABLE 6

Distribution of Anganwadis according to the Duration of Functioning

Years	Rural Area No=45	Urban Slums No=55	Total No=100
Less than 7 years	11.2	10.9	11.0
8 to 10 years	48.8	16.4	31.0
More than 11 years	40.0	72.7	58.0
Total	100.0	100.0	100.0

Thus, the majority of these anganwadis, (89%) were in operation, for a minimum period of eight years. Thirty-seven percent of these anganwadis functioned in single-room apartments, some with an attached 'veranda'. The rest all functioned in smaller buildings of varying structures. Thus there was the problem of congestion because, on an average, an anganwadi had to cater to 35 children. Interestingly, 73 percent of these anganwadis functioned in rented buildings. The rest of the anganwadis, however, had government accommodation. There was no evidence of securing community support for the IDCS programme because the rent was being charged even for those buildings which belonged to the local Panchayats. Another important aspect was that 68 percent of these anganwadis were being used for living purpose also, either by the owners of these buildings or their tenants, after the working hours (Table 7).

TABLE 7

Distribution of Anganwadis according to Selected Physical Characteristics

Characteristics	Rural Area No=45	Urban Slums No=55	Total No=100
I. Type			
Kutcha	5.5	3.6	5.0
Semi-Pucca	11.2	12.7	12.0
Pucca	67.3	83.7	83.0
II. Size			
One room	26.6	45.4	37.0
One room + Open Space	40.0	18.3	28.0
More than one room and open space	33.4	36.3	35.0
III. Building			
Government	13.3	38.1	27.0
Rented	86.7	61.9	73.0
IV. Shared by owners/Tenants			
Yes	62.2	72.7	68.0
No	37.8	37.3	32.0

TABLE 8

Distribution of Anganwadi according to Availability of Facilities

Facilities	Rural Area No=45	Urban Slums No=55	Total No=100
Electricity			
Yes	93.3	90.1	92.0
No	6.7	9.9	8.0
Water			
Piped	73.3	72.2	72.0
Hand Pumps	6.7	27.8	28.0
Latrines			
Yes	11.2	21.8	17.0
No	88.8	78.2	83.0

This had an adverse effect on the image of these anganwadis. Certain charts, concerning family planning, could not be displayed on the walls due to objections from the owners of the buildings. The rent sanctioned for an anganwadi building was so small (Rs. 120 per month) that better buildings were beyond reach. But nothing was considered as more serious a problem by the angaanwadi workers than the delayed payment of rent for the anganwadi buildings. We were told that this was a persistent irritant affecting their relationship with the landlords. In one case, a village Sarpanch was so adamant and reactive on delayed payment of rent for a Panchayat-owned anganwadi building that he threatened to close it down without even issuing a notice to the government. The general hygienic conditions of these anganwadis were far from satisfactory. Only one-fourth of them appeared upto the mark. All the rest had varying problems of hygiene and maintenance. But practically all these anganwadis were electrified, though there was the problem of erratic supply of electricity. The supply of safe drinking water to these anganwadis was also unsatisfactory because they did not have any storage facility (Table 8). None of these anganwadis could afford the luxury of having a plastic bucket for providing drinking water to the children. Some of the earthen pots, provided for keeping the drinking water, were in bad shape and they were not being replaced for inexplicable reasons. Another disturbing aspect of the anganwadi situation was that 80 percent of these anganwadis did not have the facility of a toilet. (Table 9). The children were, therefore, forced to go to fields or nearby open spaces for the purpose of urination or defecation. In case any child complained of diarrhoea, he had to be sent back home. The physical environment of the anganwandis, therefore, was not conducive to toilet training. Yet there were some advantageous aspects which should not be overlooked. Most of these anganwadis were centrally-located and thus easily accessible to the beneficiaries. There was no problem of cooking food, or, of washing dishes, as only a ready-to-eat snack was provided at the angrnwandis. In a way, this also saved the anganwadi workers from facing the problem of obtaining fuel for cooking a hot meal for the children. In the villages, timber is still being used as the main type of fuel for cooking food and this had led, to some extent, to the associated problem of deforestation. The forests provide about 62 percent of the domestic fuel for cooking or heating urban dwellings. According to one source, in the 1980s, over 250 million cubic meters of timber was cut down every year, while the estimated growth of woods was only 15 million cubic meters. The consumption was found to be five times higher than the growth. No wonder, the present forest area—22 percent—is far below the absolute minimum forest area required.

TABLE 9

Distribution of Anganwadis according to Adequacy of Available Facilities

Condition of facilities	Rural Area No=45	Urban Slums No=55	Total No=100
Water			
Adequate	11.2	18.2	15.0
Partially adequate	31.0	54.5	53.0
Not adequate	37.8	27.3	32.0
Toilet			
Adequate	5.5	27.3	18.0
Partially adequate	67.3	32.7	55.0
Not adequate	11.2	40.0	27.0
Electricity			
Adequate	33.4	36.3	35.0
Partially adequate	62.1	54.5	57.0
Not Adequate	5.5	9.2	8.0

The bulk of these anganwadis (90%) had some furnishings or equipment—usually an almirah, a dustbin, and, a couple of carpets. These anganwadis were provided with some utensils for serving food but these were lying idle. Neither the broken furniture was replaced, nor any attempt made to provide small-sized carpets so that these could be cleaned properly. Moreover, while so much stress was laid on the preparation and maintenance of records at the anganwadi, no effort was made to provide the anganwadi worker a table for writing. There was no provision for an extra chair in the anganwadi. So where would the anganwadi worker make her supervisor sit when she visits her anganwadi ? Then there was also the irksome problem of shortage of stationery. Non-availability or delayed availability of such items often forced these anganwadi workers to spend money from their own pocket to purchase them. Paying attention to such trivial matters can go a long way in improving the general conditions of these anganwadis.

Aanganwadi Workers : Some Aspects of their Role

Despite these problems, the anganwadi workers were somehow able to maintain proper records. Some of them mentioned to us that it was difficult for them to spend so much time on the preparation of vital satistics and growth charts. At the same time, data of considerable importance, on such aspects as the use of medicines by the beneficiaries ; motivational efforts made by the anganwadi workers for enhancing the immunization coverage as well as improving the referral services, were not available. In the absence of such data, it was difficult, to assess objectively, the true contribution of anganwadi workers to the health programme. Some anganwadi workers were vocal enough to inform us that they were pressurised by some health personnel to spend more time on the preparation of growth charts. Now, this activity can yieled the desired result only when there is proper follow-up action. We found no evidence of this.

We noticed that play was being considered as an important activity of these anganwadis. Through play, the children were able to learn many physical, social and intellectual skills. Besides, play provided them opportunities to learn the basic principles of living and working together. It also afforded them a chance to develop their capacities to the fullest extent. However, only 20 percent of these angwadis had some play grounds or open spaces nearby where children could play. But children were provided with a variety of toys such as aeroplanes, ducks and horses—all made of wood. Some of these anganwadis also had a 'Dholak' to be played on special occasions. Most of these anganwadis were not provided with soap, or any other detergent, for washing hands. This surprised us because of late, so much stress has been laid, in the health circles, on lack of hand washing as a contributory factor to diarrhoea. We ourselves observed many children eating bread without bothering to wash their hands, either before or after eating. The anganwadi workers were apparently helpless becaus they had no provision for handwashing within their premises. If they had allowed the children to wash hands in the open spaces, they would have further aceentuated the problem of pollution.

Undoubtedly, the anganwadi worker is the back-bone of the ICDS programme. If she is well-trained, well-supervised, and well-supported, there is no reason why she would not be able to make a good contribution to the ICDS programme. We wanted to know who these anganwadi workers were ? What kind of socio economic back-ground did they represent ? What made them join the ICDS scheme ? What were their training needs ? What contributions, did they think, they have made towards activities such as immunization, and diagnosis and treatment of minor ailments. And also what suggestions did they have for improving the functioning of the ICDS scheme ?

We found that a majority of the anganwadi workers were between the ages of 26-45 years (77%). Only 18 percent of them were less than 25, and another 5 percent, were over 46.

Thus the assumption that unmarried women would be more suitable to the ICDS scheme, because they would be free from the burden of family responsibility, does not seem to hold ground because in our study three-fourths of the anganwadi workers were married (78%). Only 14 percent of them were unmarried, and, the remaining 8 percent, were either widows or separated. In a study done by the Nutrition Foundation of India, however, a majority of the anganwadi workers were found to be unmarried In our study area, the majority of the anganwadi workers were Hindus (75%). Of the rest, 21 percent were Sikhs and another four percent, either Muslims or Christians. As regard their caste status, 47 percent of the anganwadi workers belonged to the intermediate castes, and 40 percent to the lower castes and backward classes. Over 50 percent of them came from families, having a monthly income of Rs. 2001 to 3000. (Table 10) The majority of them belonged to the joint families (62.0%). Most of the anganwadi workers had 1-2 living children (Table 11). In most cases, their husbands were in the age group 31-50. They were mostly engaged in service. (Table 12'. Interestingly, a majority of the anganwadi workers had studied upto the secondary standard. Some of them were graduates, and 52 percent with an additional diploma or certificate in technical education, such as teachers training, cutting and tailoring and stenography (Table 13) A few of the anganwadi workers seemed to have a chip on the shoulders because they were expected to leave any time they got a better job. Then there were some others who had started working for the ICDS scheme, under family compulsions. An interesting case was that of a young stenotypist, who was prevented, by her family members, from joining the government service, said, R.K. :

> "Left to myself, I would have joined the government job as a stenotypist. But my parents did not want me to work in the city as they thought any exposure to the city life was bound to mar my chances of getting a proper spouse".

TABLE 10

Distribution of Anganwadi Workers according to their Socio-economic Characteristics

Characteristics	Rural Area No=45	Urban Slums No=55	Total No=100
I. *Age Group (In Years)*			
Less than 25	17.8	18.2	18.0
26-35	44.4	47.2	46.0
36-45	33.3	29.1	31.0
46 and above	4.4	5.5	5.0
II. *Marital Status*			
Married	80.0	76.3	78.0
Unmarried	8.8	18.2	14.0
Widow/Divorced	11.2	5.5	8.0
III. *Religion*			
Hindus	80.0	70.9	75.0
Sikhs	17.8	23.6	21.0
Others	2.2	5.5	4.0
IV. *Caste*			
Higher Castes	48.8	45.4	47.0
Intermediate castes	11.2	14.6	13.0
Lower castes and backward classes	40.0	40.0	40.0
V. *Family Income (In Rupees)*			
Less than Rs. 2000	42.2	12.7	26.0
Rs. 2001 to 3000	46.6	54.5	51.0
Rs. 3001 and above	11.2	32.8	23.0

TABLE 11

Distribution of Anganwari Workers according to their Family Type and Family Size

Family Type/Size	Rural Area No=45	Urhan Slums No=55	Total No=100
I. Family Type			
Nuclear	37.8	36.6	38.0
Joint	62.2	63.4	62.0
II. Number of Living Children			
No Child	13.3	18.2	16.0*
1—2	48.9	49.1	49.0
3—4	33.3	30.9	32.0
5 and above	4.5	1.8	3.0

*Including 8 unmarried Anganwadi worners.

TABLE 12

Distribution of Anganwadi Workers according to the Husband's Age and Occupation

Age/Occupation	Rural Area No=36	Urban Slums No=42	Total No=78
Age Group (In Years)			
Less than 30	11.1	9.6	8.0
31—40	36.2	57.1	37.0
41—50	50.0	28.5	30.0
51 and above	2.7	4.8	3.0

Occupation Status			
Service			40.0
Government	44.5	57.1	20.0
Private	22.2	28.5	
Business	22.2	7.2	11.0
Other (Retired/ Unemployed etc)	11.1	7.2	7.0

TABLE 13

Distribution of Anganwadi Workers according to their Educational Status

Educational Status	Rural Area No=45	Urban Slums No=55	Total No=100
Upto 10th Standard	33.3	50.9	43.0
11—12	55.5	36.3	45.0
13th and above	11.2	12.8	12.0
Additional skills			
Yes	40.0	39.2	52.2
No	60.0	61.8	48.0

We noted that quite a good number of them had found it convenient to supplement their income by participating in income generating activities, such a tutions, tailoring, and adult education. Interestingly, 83 percent of them were not residing in villages or slums. where these anganwadis were located. But a majority of them were living closeby. Therefore, they did not face any problem of identity or alienation. Despite incurring considerable expenditure on travelling, the bulk of them appeared quite attentive to their work. (Table 14). In fact,

TABLE 14

Distribution of Anganwadi Workers according to their Place of Residence and Mode of Transport

Place/Distance Transport	Rural Area No=45	Urban Slums No=55	Total No=100
Living within	13.3	21.8	18.0
Living outside	86.7	78.2	82.0
Distance from Residence (*in kms.*)			
Living in the same village	13.3	21.8	18.0
Within 3	31.2	32.8	32.0
3 to 5	33.3	23.6	28.0
6 and above	22.2	21.8	22.0
Mode of Transport			
On Foot	22.2	27.3	25.0
On Cycle	6.6	9.1	8.0
Public Transport	55.5	58.2	37.0
Private Transport	15.7	5.4	10.0

Average Daily Expenditure			
No expenditure	13.3	21.8	18.0
Less than Rs. 3	26.6	9.1	17.0
Rs. 3 to 5	37.8	47.3	43.0
Rs. 5 and above	22.3	21.8	22.0

some of them could be singled out for examplary performance in the face of petty annoyances. For example, there was Mrs. S. a 28 years old woman, who regularly cycled down to her anganwadi, covering a distance of 8 to 10 kms. And she was rarely found late. The important thing was the interest shown by this young woman, with a rural background, in serving the anganwadi. We found that despite constraints, a large number of them remained stuck to their duties for more than six years (Table 15) Undoubtedly, these key persons, at the grassroots

TABLE 15

Distribution of Anganwadi Workers according to their Work Experience as Anganwadi Worker

Experience	Rural Area No=45	Urban Slums No=55	Total No=100
Less than 5 years	17.8	18.2	18.0
6--10 years	55.5	54.5	55.0
11 years and above	26.7	27.3	27.0

level were making a valuable contribution to the functioning of the ICDS scheme. They provided enough evidence of their willingnesss to contribute to the ICDS scheme in their varied situations. They were the kind of change agents whose voice was heard with respect and whose words were trusted by the people. In any case, they had proved themselves to be free from any kind of suspicion on the part of the people. They were not like those 'outsiders' who represented a different cultural background and maintained a distance from the people. The local anganwadi workers, however, had greater plus points to their credit. They had the advantage of knowing the people better and of identifying the key persons and organizations whose help and support they could seek for the implementation of the ICDS scheme. Needless to say that proper relationship and interaction with the local people were necessary for the smooth functioning of the scheme. The following case would reveal how a non-resident anganwadi worker had adjusted on her assigned role :

> Mrs. R.K. 38, belongs to a backward class family. She has been working as an anganwadi worker for the past ten years. She joined the ICDS scheme as an anganwadi worker on the insistence of her father-in-law. Initially, she worked in her husband's village for about eight months. But then she got herself transferred to a neighbouring village. The reason was that some members of her family openly objected to her going from house-to-house, urging people to send their children to the anganwadi. Working in a neighbouring village was devoid of any such problems and she, in fact, found it more convenient to adjust.

What were their reasons for joining the ICDS scheme? Most anganwadi workers were frank enough to admit that they had joined the scheme on economic considerations. However, there were others who said that they joined the scheme purely for serving the children. We noticed that the weightage given to economic factor was somewhat on the higher side. The humanitarian factor weighed heavily with less than one-third of the anganwadi workers (Table 16). But then we must hasten to add

TABLE 16

Distribution of Anganwadi Workers according to their main Reason for Joining as an Anganwadi Worker

Reason	Rural Area No=45	Urban Slums No=55	Total No=100
I. Economic	80.0	78.0	79.0
II. To serve the community	20.0	21.8	21.0

that many of those who had joined the ICDS scheme on economic considerations, had developed so much interest in serving the children that they were not inclined to seek alternate positions. The following cases may throw some light on this aspect :

Says P.L. :

'I joined the scheme with the main purpose of serving the children. I find my work very interesting and absorbing and I have not faced any problem or inconvenience in the performance of my duties, I have been on this job for more than ten years. I am a trained teacher with a diploma in stitching and tailoring. Had I wanted to change, I would have done it long ago. I have no intention of giving up my present position. It would be nice if some additional facilities are provided to us at the anganwadi. As far as I am concerned, nothing would deter me from performing my duties at the anganwadi to the best of my ability ?

Says T.L. :

'Others may call me temperamental but I have an innate

desire to serve my people, especially the children. I am a graduate, and, if I wanted, I would have got another job. I have taken up this position because I want to do social work. It's nice being in the company of young children, playing with them, feeding them, and teaching them certain basic things in life. For me, the children are like little plants. I take care of them like a gardener. I like them to grow. Where else, could I find such an opportunity to fulfil my inner desires."

Says K.K. :

'I am a widow with two children. I have joined the anganwadi both for social and economic reasons. Socially, my family members have liked my working here because this work is free from social problems. And economically, I make some money to provide for the needs of my children. Even otherwise, I feel satisfied. I must say that now even a day's absence from the anganwadi makes me feel bored'.

Says M.K. :

"After separation from my husband, I thought, I should do something to keep myself busy. Working with the children helps me in my personal adjustment and keeps me free from loneliness and boredem. I have no desire to seek any other work. So, come what may, I am not likely to leave my present position".

What did they think about their capability to perform their duties ? The bulk of them were of the view that they needed further training to perform their duties better (Table 17). They were able to spell out their training requirements without much difficulty. The areas in which they required training were : (i) diagnosis and treatment of minor ailments ; (ii) signs and symptoms of different grades of malnutrition (iii) food values

TABLE 17

Distribution of Anganwadi Workers according to their Perception of their Role Performance

Performance of duty	Roral Area No=45	Urban Slums No=55	Total No=100
I. Can perform duties adequately	24.4	29.1	27.0
II. Would need further training to perform duties adequately	75.6	70.9	73.0

of locally available foods ; (iv) pregnancy-related health problems ; (v) local beliefs about health and nutrition ; and (vi) environmental problems affecting health. (Table 18). We may mention here that 61 percent of them had already undergone re-orientation training. (Table 19). But all of them expressed the feeling that this training was deficient. Perhaps no one would disagree that the anganwadi workers were in need of further training. The major issue was how to plan their training covering all the relevant aspects. Needless to say that there was a great need to develop a culturally acceptable training progromme for the anganwadi workers. This task could be accomplished better by a team of specialists representing the medical and social science disciplines. Obviously, if these anganwadi workers were imparted further training, there was every possibility of improvement in their role performance. We may also state here that some anganwadi workers were very particular in pinpointing to us some of their personal problems. Their trainers, therefore, would do well if they understood all of their problems before offering them any practical solutions. Actually, when the problems of grassroots level workers get accentuated and solutions are delayed, all one can expect is chaos.

TABLE 18

Distribution of Anganwadis according to their Opinions about Areas Requiring More Training

Areas requiring Training	Rural Area No=45	Urban Slums No=55	Total No=100
Diagnosis and Treatment of ailments	64.4	63.6	64.0
Detection of Pregnancy related health problems-	57.7	54.5	56.0
Use of growth monitoring charts	44.4	49.1	47.0
Filling up of records	40.0	36.3	38.0
Nutritive values of foods	37.7	34.5	36.0
Securing community participation	33.3	25.5	29.0

TABLE 19

Distribution of Anganwadi Workers according to their Reorientation Training

Training	Rural Area No=45	Urban Slums No=55	Total No=100
Had undergone reorientation training	51.1	69.1	61.1
Had not undergone reorientation training	48.9	30.9	39.0

What about the impact of the ICDS scheme? What did the anganwadi workers themselves think about it? Again, the anganwadi workers response to such querries was as clear as one could expect. The majority of them (71.0%) were of the view that the ICDS scheme had a good effect on the existing programmes and activities in terms of (i) increasing the immunisation coverage ; (ii) reducing the present school drop-out rate; (iii) reducing the infant mortality rate and (iv) reducing the incidence of malnutrition. In addition, they also perceived that the ICDS scheme and enhanced the awareness of the mothers about the value of : (i) health check-up for their children ; (ii) use of safe drinking water had (iii) better child care in a small family. (Table 20) Interestingly, the bulk

TABLE 20

Distribution of Anganwadis workers according to their own perception about the impact of ICDS programme

Impact of ICDS in the Area	Rural Area No=45	Urban Slums No=55	Total No=100
A. Reduction in			
(i) Maternal mortality	40.0	49.1	55.0
(ii) Incidence of Malnutrition	33.3	41.8	48.8
(iii) Infant mortality	37.7	42.7	46.0
(iv) School dropouts	46.6	43.9	45.0
(v) Incidence of anaemia	26.6	23.6	25.0

B. Increased Awareness About

(i) Immunisation	57.7	63.6	71.0
(ii) Having small family	51.1	61.8	58.0
(iii) Health check-up	42.2	50.9	47.0
(iv) Maintaining cleanliness	35.5	43.6	40.0
(v) Eating of Proper Food	22.2	21.8	22.0

of the anganwadi workers were continuing on the job with the hope of getting a better honrarium (Table 21). But the same

TABLE 21

Distribution of Anganwadis workers according to their Reasons for Continuation on Present Job

Reasons for Continuation	Rural Area No=45	Urban Slums No=55	Total No=100
(i) Hoping to get better honrarium	68.8	70.9	70.0
(ii) Hoping to become permanent Govt. employee	60,0	67.3	65,0
(iii) Wants to serve the community	26.6	29.1	28.0

was not true of their helpers whose socio-economic background was different (Tables 22-23). A scrutiny of records had revealed

TABLE 22

Socio-Demographic Characteristics of Helpers

Characteristics	Rural Area No=45	Urban Area No=55	Total No=100
I. Age Group (In Years)			
Less than 25	4.4	5.5	5.0
26—35	33.3	45.6	40.0
36—45	44.5	40.0	42.0
46 and above	17.8	9.9	13.0
II. Marital Status			
Married	84.4	92.8	89.0
Unmarried	8.8	3.6	6.0
Widows	6.6	3.6	5.0
III. Religion			
Hindus	77.7	76.4	77.0
Sikhs	15.6	18.1	17.0
Others	6.7	5.5	6.0
IV. Caste Status			
Higher castes	26.6	27.3	27.0
Middle castes	17.8	20.0	19.0
Lower and backward castes	55.6	52.7	54.0

V. Educational Status			
Illiterate	66.7	49,1	57.0
Literate	33.3	50.9	43.0
VI. Family Income			
Less than Rs. 1000	53.4	29.1	40.0
Rs. 1001—1500	33.3	49.1	42.0
Rs. 1500 and above	13.3	21.8	18.0

TABLE 23

Distribution of Anganwadi Helpers according to their Family Type and Size

Type/Size	Rural Area No=45	Urban Area No=55	Total No=100
I. Family Type			
Nuclear	33.3	49.1	42.0
Joint	66.7	50.9	58.0
II. Family Size			
No child	11.1	5.4	8.0
1—2 children	15.5	9.1	12.8
3—4 children	68.8	72.7	71.0
5 and above children	26.6	12.8	19.0

III. Place of Residence			
Within the village	84.4	89.1	87.0
Outside the village	15.6	11.9	13.0

that there was indeed improvement in relation to particular activities such as immunisation coverage and control of childhood malnutrition. However, we had no way to assess the extent to which these positive changes were due to the efforts of anganwadi workers alone. The present recording system had no provision for covering some of the most important though ill-defined aspects of the role performance of the anganwadi workers.

What were some of the measureable achievements of these anganwadis ? We found that a population of 95, 160 (56.6% males and 43.4% females) was being covered by these 100 anganwadis. The coverage of male population was relatively higher in urban slums than in rural areas (urban slums : 59.9%; rural areas : 53.3%) (Table 24) As many as 1678 pregnant

TABLE 24

Sex-Wise Distribution of Population in the Anganwadis

Type of Anganwadis	Population covered Male	Female	Total
Rural Area	25651 (53.3)	22490 (46.7)	48141 (100.0)
Urban Slums	28179 (59.9)	18840 (40,1)	47019 (100.0)
Total	53133 (56.6)	41330 (43.4)	95160 (100.0)

women were identified in the covered population. Of these, only 1041 pregnant women were enrolled at the 100 anganwadis. The majority of them i.e. 1,010 pregnant women were receiving supplementary nutrition. In contrast, only 919 lactating mothers, out of a total of 1863 lactating mothers identified, were enrolled at the anganwadis and they were all receiving supplementary nutrition (Table 25). In addition, 6826 children were covered, of whom, 42.6 percent

TABLE 25

Distribution of Pregnant and Lactating Women in the Anganwadis

Type of Anganwadis	Pregnant Women in the Area	Enrolled	Receiving	Nursing Women in the Area	Enrolled	Receiving
Rural Area	961 (57.3)	563 (54.1)	540 (53.4)	1056 (59.2)	504 (54.8)	504 (54.8)
Urban Slums	717 (42.7)	478 (45.9)	470 (46.6)	727 (40.8)	415 (45.2)	415 (45.2)
Total	1678 (100.0)	1041 (100.0)	1010 (100.0)	1883 (100.0)	919 (100.0)	919 (100.0)

were between six months to three years and 57.4 percent between 3 years to 6 years (Table 26). Nutritionally, 49.2 percent were considered normal, while 34.6 percent were in Grade I, 15.6 in Grade II and only 0.6 percent in Grade III (Table 27). We were able to collect some data pertaining to children from selected anganwadis. These data

TABLE 26

Age-wise Distribution of Children in the Anganwadis

Age Group	Rural Area	Urban Slums	Total
6 months to 3 years	1148 (39.4)	1762 (60.6)	2910 (42.6)
3 years to 6 years	1832 (40.1)	2084 (53.2)	3916 (57.4)
Total	2980 (100.0)	3846 (100.0)	6826 (100.0)

TABLE 27

Nutritional Status of Children in the Age Group 3—6 Years in the Anganwadis

Nutritional Status	Rural Area	Urban Slums	Total
Normal	982 (53.6)	944 (45.2)	1926 (49.2)
Grade-I	628 (34.3)	730 (35.1)	1358 (34.6)
Grade-II	215 (11.7)	393 (18.9)	610 (15.6)

Grade.III	7 (0.4)	15 (0.7)	22 (0.6)
Total	1832 (100.0)	2084 (100.0)	3916 (100.0)

showed that of the 1790 enrolled children, between the ages 6 months to 3 years, only 590 children were receiving supplementary nutrition. On the other hand, of the 2067 enrolled children, in the age group 3-6 years, only 860 children were receiving supplementary nutrition. In a situation like this, it was difficult to identify developmental deficiencies among children who were not covered by the ICDS scheme. We may point out that children below the age of three years are often very creative and imaginative. Missing them at this stage may amount to a denial of opportunity for development. To be more precise, it may mean a denial of chance to develop creativity in the company of other children. It is important that all children in an anganwadi area are provided many outlets for satisfaction of their urges to create, to learn, and to develop. In our observation, the home of an average scheduled caste child was hard-pressed to accommodate his exploratory drives. The anganwadi would certainly be a good substitute for a deficient home.

We noted that only a ready-to-eat snack was distributed to the children at these 100 anganwadis. This food was supplied to children below the age of six years for 300 days a year. We were told that this ready-to-eat snack contained the ingredients similar to those found in the cooked food provided in other anganwadis. The anganwadi workers were expected to make a special effort to enroll all children below the age of three years. They were expected to contact their parents and siblings for this purpose. As mentioned earlier, supplementary feeding was to bridge the caloric gap. We noted that all the 100 anganwadis regularly received the packets of 'special bread' for distribution. The daily supply of bread packets ranged from 8 packets to 16 packets. (Table 28) We were able to observe the pattern of

TABLE 28

Distribution of Anganwadis according to the Number of Packets of bread Consumed

Number of Packets of bread consumed	Rural Area No=45	Urban Slums No=55	Total No=10o
Less than 8	28.9	21.8	25.0
9—11	26.6	27.3	27.0
12—14	22.2	27.3	25.0
15—16	22.2	23.6	21.0

bread distribution and bread consumption by the children in some anganwadis. We found that about 50 percent of the children did not consume the bread supplied to them at the anganwadis, instead they carried it to their homes. We were not able to identify the extent to which it was wasted during the interval between the supply and consumption. But, two reasons were given by some of the anganwadi workers for carrying the bread home—one, because it was easy for the child to take it with a cup of milk or tea at home, and, second, because the families of the beneficiaries were able to confirm that the snack was actually provided to their children.

One of the objectives of the ICDS programme was to get the expectant and nursing mothers examined at regular intervals by the lady health visitor (LHV) and Auxiliary Nurse Midwife (ANM). This was done with the purpose of diagnosing minor ailments and distributing simple medicines. The anganwadi workers were to act as link persons between the villagers and the health team. In this regard, our findings revealed that the majority of the anganwadis were visited by the ANMs at least once, during the past three months, for health check-up of expectant and nursing mothers. In contrast, the lady health visitor (LHV) made only 7 visits and the Medical Officer only 4 visits. But practically, all the anganwadis were visited, at least twice a month, by the Mukhya Sevikas. A CDPO visit to the anganwadi was a rare phenomenon. We noted that the stress on health and nutrition education of pregnant and lactating mothers was far from satisfactory. The anganwadi workers had adopted a casual approach towards this activity. Even an important activity like home visiting was not given due importance. The bulk of their time got consumed in the preparation of charts and maintenance of records. We also made an effort to find out as to how did they use the medicine kit that was provided to them. We found that, on an average, each anganwadi worker, had treated 7 cases in one month, prior to our interview. (Table 29) Thus a total of 696 cases were treated by these 100 anganwadi workers during a period of one month. The cases treated by them, ranged from worm infestations to cough and cold. (Table 30) We were told that the supply of drugs was quite erratic. Yet, only 8 of them had fully utilized all the medicines provided to them. According to them, there was a great need for medicines for the treatment of common illnesses such as cough and cold, skin infections, diarrhoea and gastric disorders. (Table 31).

TABLE 29

Distribution of Anganwadi Workers according to the Number of Cases Treated during the Last One Month

Number of cases treated	Rural Area No=45	Urban Slums No=55	Total No=100
Less than 5	18.0	21.8	21.0
6—8	44.4	47.3	46.0
9—10	31.1	21.8	26.0
11 and more	4.4	9.1	7.0

TABLE 30

Distribution of Anganwadi Workers according to the Type of cases treated by them during the Last One Month

Type of cases	Rural Area No—272	Urban Slums No=424	Total No=696
Fever	22.1	18.8	20.1
Cough and Cold	11.1	12.9	12.2
Diarrhoea	4.8	6.5	5.7
Boils/Cuts/Wounds	14.6	5.9	9.3

Worm infestations	14.6	14.7	14.6
Skin Infections	11.7	13.6	12.9
Stomach disorders	8.5	2.8	5.1
Eye Infections	6.7	11.2	9.3
Earache	2.2	9.3	6.4
Bodyache/weakness	0.8	4.2	2.8
Others	2.9	0.2	1.3

TABLE 31

Distribution of Anganwadi Workers according to their Additional Requirements of Drugs

Drugs needed	Rural Area No -45	Urban Siums No=55	Total No=100
(i) Septran	66.6	45.4	55.0
(ii) Chloroquine	48.8	36.3	42.0
(iii) Multivitamins	37.7	41.8	40.0
(iv) B. Complex	28.8	45.5	38.0
(v) Cough Syrup	22.2	45.5	35.0
(vi) Benzyl Benzoate	26.5	23.6	25.0
(vii) Oral Rehydration Salt	13.3	32.7	24.0

From the consideration of children, a continuing dependable relationship with a soft-spoken anganwadi worker, like the one whose case study we have described in the next chapter, is important for several reasons. One reason is that during the first few years of life, a child needs to develop a sense of trust in someone who can help him become aware of his immediate environment and feel secure in the company of others. He needs to know that he is liked. At the anganwadi, therefore, he needs something more than mere feeding or singing of a few songs. In other words, he is clearly in need of a variety of experiences that are conducive to his development. An honest and dedicated anganwadi worker can certainly provide him these opportunities. We need hardly to stress that the children who are brought up in an impersonal environment may become apathetic in later life. A child's association with the anganwadi should, therefore, provide him highly stimulating experiences. This is essential particularly in the case of those children whose parents are less likely to provide them a stimulating environment. In fact, a sensitive anganwadi worker should consider the differential needs of boys and girls. After all, boys and girls tend to be quite different in their patterns of growth and development. Some experts feel that boys are more vulnerable to physical and emotional stress than girls. They say that boys may require greater attention when they are under stress. It has also been stated that differences in the ways that boys and girls develop generally become more marked as children get older. And as explained by us earlier, these differences could be of a biological or a cultural origin. The subculture of a scheduled caste child is vastly different from the subculture of a higher caste child.

5

Case Study of an Anganwadi Worker

Mrs. B.K., is in her early 30. She is a woman of independent nature. She has studied upto the inter-mediate standard, got married and has two children. She does not consider herself to be an appendage of her husband. Her purpose in life is not merely to fulfill the needs and desires of her husband but to live a life of her own liking, of her own dreams. When I met her for the first time, she was wearing a bright yellow dress—a salwar kameez combination—which highlighted her wheatish complexion and sparkling eyes. She was sitting on a trunk in a small room where about 30 children had assembled for the day's activities. I sat next to her in a partly broken chair to talk to her about her work in the Anganwadi.

The anganwadi functions in a one-room building which is electrified and well-ventilated. It has plenty of open space for children to play. A handpump installed nearby provides them safe drinking water. But, like many other anganwadis, it lacks the basic facility of a toilet. It has a few belongings—a chair, a trunk, an almirah, a weighing machine, a carpet and a few untensils. It also has a some toys made of locally available material. Several registers containing information about the performance of its various activities are also available. There is a daily attendance register, a stock register, a copy of daily work and growth chart. But the 'guide book' and other manuals are not available. A few charts that have been supplied are not in a proper condition to be hung on the walls. So the room gives an empty look. The anganwadi covers 214 families or a population of 1002. On an average, it caters to 35 children, between the ages of 3 to 6 years, in addition to covering 19 children, between the ages of 6 months to 3 years. It functions for four-and-a-half hours on all working days, except the holidays. About 8 packets of bread are distributed to children, pregnant women and nursing mothers everyday. On one occasion when the bread packets were being distributed, I noticed two well-fed rats moving in and out of the room without causing any alam among the children. I was told that rats sometimes consume the leftover parts of the bread supplied to the beneficiaries. There was certainly some wastage of bread. We hear that over 15 million tonnes of grains are annually consumed by rats in India and the losses, as per one estimate, are 4.5 blliion rupees. At another anganwadi, in Raipur Rani Community Development Block of Haryana, a variety of locally-cooked food preparations were offered to the beneficiaries. This approach had attracted a lot more children to the anganwadi.

The day starts with a small prayer by the children, seeking the blessings of God for becoming good citizens. This is followed by simple physical exercises and other activities such as health check-up and feeding. The children sit together, sing and play in a cordial atmosphere. The songs sung by them stimulate them enormously, raising their curiosity about the would around them. We have recorded some of their songs. The two popular songs are proffered here to give the readers an idea about the massage they carry.

I

Mein Niki Jhai Munni,
Mere Sir Pe Lal Chunni,
Mera Sitarian Wala Suit,
Mere Nike Nike Boot,
Mein Anganwadi Vich Pardi Haan,
Sab Nun Piyari Lagdi Haan,
Sab Nun Ta Ta Kardi Haan,

(I am a litle girl,
I wear a red head gear,
I wear a dotted suit,
And tiny tiny boots,
Anganwadi is my school,
I am loved by all,
I say Ta Ta to all.

II

Golam Ghol, Pahi Golam Ghol,
Dada Ji Ka Danda Ghol,
Dadi Ji Ki Ainak Ghol,
Mummi Ji Ki Roti Ghol,
Daddy Ji Ka Paisa Ghol,
Bache Kehte Laddu Ghol,
Madam Kehti Sari Dunya Ghol.

(Round and round, round and round,
Grandpa's rod is round,
Grandma's spects are round,
Mumma's bread is round,
Daddy's coin is round,
Children say candy is round,
Teacher says the world is round).

She was articulate and confident. But she was soft-spoken, her speech slow, and her voice unlike a typical Punjabi girl. She was a determined person with a mind of her own, for what she told me was quite revealing of her inner strengths. I was struck by her determination to work for the welfare of poor children. Says she : "I am not like those women who live under a perpetual sort of house arrest because of their confinement to a busy routine throughout the day. I like to work here because I feel independent and I gain the same respect as other working women in Chandigarh. Actually, when I learnt about the possibility of my working here, I was quite excited. I felt the anganwadi had offered me a much-needed opportunity to be free from a boring household routine. I no longer needed to spend my whole day in cooking and cleaning household utensils. Luckily, I had an opportunity to go to the school and that is why today I can read and write. Now, I try to stimulate the children of my anganwadi, arouse their curiosity by involving them in innovative plays and games, so that when they grow up, they could discover the world on their own".

Today, the lives of many anganwadi workers like her, are unlike the lives of their mothers and grandmothers. This is not to say that they are no longer wedded to the old customs and habits. Their respect for the old tradition is seen in the way they relate to each other. Says she : "I feel, I am not independent economically of my husband just because I earn a little money here. In praetically every respect, all my behaviour has to be approved by my husband. Actually, I had a different degree of independence before my marriage. I think, the freest part of my life was from the time I was a youngster until I got married. Nevertheless, I feel that my work here has enabled me to serve a good cause. I look after the needs of poor children—their health, nutritional and educational needs. I meet their mothers and also pregnant women and nursing mothers in the village and try to help them. They, in turn, extend me whatever help they can in my work".

A close scrutiny of the records maintained at the anganwadi enabled us understand the role performance of this anganwadi worker at two specific points in a year-January and December. For instance, in January, 1991, we found that the anganwadi worker was able to identify fifteen pregnant women in her assigned work area and population. However, only four of them could be enrolled by her at the anganwadi. They were regularly receiving nutrition supplementation. By December 1991, the situation had changed somewhat in the sense that there were only eight pregnant women in her area, of whom four were attending the anganwadi. More or less a similar picture emerged in regard to the enrolment of lactating mothers.

Pregnant and lactating women enrolled at the Anganwadi, during January and December, 1991.

Type of women	Number of women		Receiving services
	Area	Enrolled	
Pregnant			
January	15	4	4
December	8	4	4
Lactating			
January	5	4	4
December	15	9	9

As regard enrolment of children, between 6 months and 3 years, it was noted that in January 1991, the anganwadi worker was able to identify 80 children, of whom, only 23 could be enrolled at the anganwadi. In contrast, in December, 1991, the number of children in this age group had increased to 89, but only 29 of them were enrolled at the anganwadi. Also, in January 199, of the 80 children identified, between 3 years and 6 years, the actual benefeciaries were only 30. In comparison, by December, 1991, while the number of children, in this age group, rose to 104, the beneficiaries were only 35.

Children enrolled at the Anganwadi, during January and December, 1991.

Age Group of Children

6 months to 3 years			
Months	Number in Area	Number Enrol.	Number Receiving Services
January	80	30	26
December	89	29	19

3 yrs. to 6 years			
Months	Number in Area	Number Enrol.	Number Receiving Services
January	80	37	30
December	104	40	35

An idea about the fluctuations in the nutritional status of children enrolled at the anganwadi can be had from the Table given below :

Age-wise distribution of children, according to their nutritional status, during January and December, 1991.

Age-Group	Normal	Grade I	Grade II	Grade III	Total
6 months to 3 years					
January	20	15	—	—	35
December	13	17	5	—	35
3 years to 6 years					
January	8	12	—	—	20
December	9	6	4	—	19

These data, at best, can throw some light on the use of growth monitoring as a technique for nutritional assessment, at the anganwadi level. Evaluating the impact of supplementary feeding on the nutritional status of children, however, is no easy task. It would indeed require a full-fledged, longitudinal study, the kind of work that has been done under the Johns Hopkins University sponsored projects in rural Punjab.

We were curious to understand the nature of functional linkages that existed between the social welfare and health departments. We made an attempt to record the total number of visits paid to this anganwadi by different categories of supervisors, during the year, 1991. We thought this kind of information would enable us understand the pattern of supervision at the grassoorts level. We were flabbergasted to know that this anganwadi was not visited even once by the Child Development Project Officer throughout 1991. The Medical Officer, however did care to visit it twice. But the maximum number of visits to the anganwadi were made by the Mukhyia Sevika (14 times). The Auxiliary Nurse Midwife, however, visited it five times. In contrast, the Lady Health Visitor had not visited the anganwadi even once. Table giving month-wise information on the visits made by the supervisors to the anganwadi, during 1991.

Month	Mukhiya Sevika	Visits by Staff			
		ANM	LHV	Medical Officer	CDPO
Jan.	1	1	—	—	—
Feb.	2	—	—	—	—
March	3	1	—	—	—
April	1	1	—	—	—
May	—	—	—	—	—
June	1	1	—	—	—
July	—	1	—	1	—
Aug.	1	—	—	1	—
Sept.	1	—	—	—	—
Oct.	2	—	—	—	—
Nov.	1	—	—	—	—
Dec.	1	—	—	—	—
Total	14	5	—	2	—

Obviously, the functional linkage between the social welfare and health departments was developing at its own sweet pace. During our field work, we learnt that this linkage was affected, to some extent, due to an unfortunate incident involving a medical officer and an anganwadi worker-cum-leader of the area. We were told that a few months ago, there was a wordy duel between the two as a result of which no medical officer had visited the anganwadi, even once, after August 1991.

During our field investigations, we were able to gather valuable information on how the anganwadi worker handled some malnourished children, enrolled at the anganwadi. A few cases, described below, would acquaint the readers with the actual field situation.

CASE ONE

"S.K. a four-and-a-half-year old, girl is the third child of a poor scheduled caste family. Her father works as a plumber in a local shop, on a small salary. His income is insufficient to provide even the basic necessities of his five-member family. S.K. joined the anganwadi on May I, 1991. On August 5, 1991, when her weight was taken, (at the age of 47 months) it was found to be only 11.5 kgs. Thus she was categorized as a Grade I malnourished child. Her history reveals that she was down with fever for nine days. This had an adverse effect on her health as during this period, she was unable to attend the anganwadi. However, later on, she became more regular and, when on 18-11-1991, her weight was taken, she had already gained 1 kg. of weight. Thus, she was able to regain the status of a 'normal' child. According to the anganwadi worker, "the improvement in her nutritional status was due to the combined effect of proper care and feeding, both at her home, and, at the anganwadi".

CASE TWO

R.S., was born on 14-9-87. He belongs to a poor Ramdasia family. His father holds a petty job in a government office and his income is hardly enough to provide a sequare meal to all members of his family. His weight record shows that he was a normal child when he joined the anganwadi—his weight was 13 kg. on 10-12-90, when he was 39 months old, and 13.5 kgs. on 10-5-91, when he was 44 months old. Then he contacted measles, which prevented him from attending the anganwadi for twelve days. According to the anganwadi worker, "his mother did take some paracetamol tablets from the anganwadi to bring down his temperature. But the moment she found out that he had measles, she refused to give him any medicine". So, on 18-11-91, when his weight was taken, it was found that he had lost 0.5 kg. of weight (at that time, he was 50 months old). Thus he had to be categorized as a Grade I malnourished child. But constant care and feeding at the anganwadi had its own reward. So when he was weighed again, after a gap of three months, he had already gained half-a-kg of weight. He was, therefore, relieved of the stigma of a malnourished child. Says the anganwadi worker: "the deterioration in his health was because of measles. Had he been properly fed during his sickness, he would have definitely, recovered fast".

CASE THREE

M.L., is about five years old. He belongs to a poor scheduled caste family. When he joined the Anganwadi, he was already quite weak and fragile. He was categorized as a Grade II malnourished child. As a result of feeding at the anganwadi there was some improvement in his health, as revealed by his weight taken on 18-11-91 (12.5 kg, at 51 months). However, he was still a Grade I malnourished child. He was being looked after well at the anganwadi. The anganwadi worker states rather aptimisfically, "he is showing definite signs of improvement".

CASE FOUR

A.K.. is a 22 months old child of an underpriviledged scheduled caste family. Despite poverty, his parents were quite alert about getting him immunized against the six preventable diseases. As per the records available with anganwadi worker, on 28-6-90, he had received BCG and three doses of Polio and D.P.T. He had also been given vaccination against measles, on 31-1-91. In May 1991, he was categorized as Grade I malnourished child as his weight was only 8.5 kg when he was 14 months old. But because of constant care and feeding, there was a definite increase in his body weight (12.5 kgms at 20 months). Accordingly he was labelled as a "normal" child.

This is indeed a glaring example of the protective and developmental role performed by the anganwadi.

The following points emerge from our analysis of this case study :

(i) that the anganwadi worker possessed considerable motivation, knowledge and skills, coupled with a desire to serve the poor people, especially the vulnerable members of the community, such as children, pregnant women and nursing mothers ;

(ii) that the anganwadi worker had the potential to expand her role further, provided she was imparted need-based training as well as given support in the performance of her duties ;

(iii) that the anganwadi worker did not show any sign of alienation from her "original constituency". On the contrary, she proved herself to be a useful 'link' person between the departments of social welfare and health as well as some other organizations ;

(iv) that the anganwadi worker did not make a good enough effort to secure community participation in the ICDS programme ;

(v) that the anganwadi worker did not plan any health or nutrition education programme for the pregnant women because she lacked proper information on the people's beliefs and practices related to health and nutrition;

(vi) that the anganwadi worker received inadequate support in her work from her senior supervisors, like the local Medical Officer and Child Development Project Officer;

(vii) that the anganwadi lacked the basic facility of a toilet ; and

(viii) that the lack of variety in food preparation being served sometimes led to 'nutritional boredom' among children, apart from food wastage.

One of the problems in the health sector is that even after effective preventive measures against certain prevalent diseases have been developed, all groups in the population have not taken advantage of them. Thus the burden of preventable illness is not reduced to the desired extent. An alert anganwadi worker, like the one described here, can certainly play a pivotal role in the adoption of preventive measures against prevalent childhood illnesses. This is because of her rapport with the people. After all, the management of childhood illnesses involves frequent and sustained alterations in the life styles of poor families. It is necessary for the anganwadi worker to be aware of the life style of beneficiaries, their habits, beliefs and practices—as this may also influence the outcome of interventions. In fact, one can make good use of such information on occasions like 'well baby clinics', medical camps, and 'health melas'. One has to realise that without people's motivation and active participation in health programmes, not much can be achieved by way of attacking the prevalent diseases. The need of the hour is to develop positive rather than negative conceptions of health. People need to be motivated to live more healthfully. Such an approach would be in conformity with the definition of health given by the World Health Organization as "a state of complete physical, mental, and social well-being, and not merely the absence of disease and infirmity". We need hardly stress here that the various commonly prevalent diseases, especially in villages and urban slums, are not caused by a single, easily identifiably agent, but seem rather to be the product of several interacting factors. Thus one has to look beyond a specific individual with a disease to the occurrence and distribution of the disease in a larger group, representing a caste, subcaste or class. Reliable clues to causes of diseases can be found through systematic observation of customs, habits, rituals and other cultural practices of the people. The anganwadi workers can play an important role in this sphere because they come in regular contact with a variety of people representing different sections of the community. In fact, the causes of diseases have been attributed to many phenomena. Perhaps what we should emphasise is that the diseases that are known to be caused by parasites, viruses and other bacteriological agents, are also influenced by environmental factors, including the factors in social environment. It is important therefore to recognize that certain environmental conditions enable some disease causing agents to flourish and others to die. With the availability of advanced technologies, all-out efforts should be made to protect our children from the prevalent diseases. We have learnt from our own experience that within the same geographical area, there are substantial differences between the rates of mortality and morbidity, especially among children. Needless to say that the privileged sections of the society in Chandigarh enjoy much better health facilities than their underprivileged counterparts residing in villages and urban slums.

6

A Model for Planning Health and Nutrition Education for Pregnant Women

An essential component of the ICDS programme is to provide care to the pregnant women, combined with health and nutrition education. In order to achieve optimum results through the education process, all faces of the programme would need to be coordinated. And this coordination, both within the ICDS system and the health system should be such that the beneficiaries can take full advantage of the knowledge, skills, and resources of these two coordinating agencies. Specialized knowledge of senior consultants and other health professionals should therefore be applied in such a way that it contributes maximally to improving the health and nutritional status of pregnant women, on whom depends the development of their children.

In planning for health and nutrition education for pregnant women, the following aspects would require special attention :

(i) the beliefs of pregnant women about etiology, diagnosis

and therapy of diseases of women and children and their perceptions about food prescriptions and proscriptions in specific disease situations ;

(ii) the pregnant women's environment—physical, biologic and social ;

(iii) the pregnant women's physiological and psychological make-up ;

(iv) the pregnant women's past experience of interacting with the health personnel and ;

(v) the rapport of anganwadi workers with the pregnant women.

A general plan for health and nutrition education can then be developed to suit the needs of all pregnant women in the anganwadi area. Actually, their needs for health and nutrition education should be re-assessed periodically as these would change gradually, depending upon such factors as changes in pregnant women's knowledge and abilities.

In addition, it might be useful to gather information on other aspects of pregnant women's life-style such as :

(i) What age is she and from what social background does she come ?

(ii) How many children has she ?

(iii) How old are they ?

(iv) What sort of paid work does she do ?

(v) How strennous is her work ?

(vi) Is her work likely to have a bad effect on the course of her pregnancy or childbirth ?

(vii) In what sort of house does she live ?

(viii) What sort of neighbourhood does she have ?

(ix) Do other women in her neighbourhood work outside the home during pregnancy ?

(x) At what stage of pregnancy does she work outside the home ?

(xi) What reasons prompted her to go out for work ? and

(xii) Is she "a pregnant woman" at risk ?

For instance, during the course of our interviews with some pregnant women, we were able to understand the complexity of factors prompting them to go out to work. The following two casses may throw some light on this aspect :

CASE ONE

Mrs. K. is a scheduled caste woman from an urban slum who is pregnant for seven months but she considers it absolutely essential for her to go out to work full-time in order to supplement her husband's income and to provide the necessities of life for her family. She leaves her three children in the house with an elderly lady from the neighbourhood to look after them during her absence. Left to herself, she would not have liked to have another child. But then being a shy person, she did not know where to get help for practising family planning. She has not visited the anganwadi in her village even once though she is aware of its existence. The anganwadi timings are unsuitable to her. In a situation like this, the anganwadi worker can help her only when she visits her home at a time when she is available.

CASE TWO

> Mrs. P belongs to a backward class rural family. After giving birth to four children, she has again become pregnant. She goes out to work on a part-time basis. The pressure of her family circumstances is such that she cannot afford to sit at home without paid work. She lives in a semi-pucca house in a neighbourhood where most houses are pucca. She desires to have a better standard of living provided her family income increases. She is hopeful of giving birth to another child. The local dai has already predicted the sex of her new-born. She is in the sixth month of pregnancy and has experienced symptoms such as headache and pain in the abdominal region. She needs help from the anganwadi worker provided such help is given to her at her place. She has heard about the local anganwadi but she has never visited it.

Obviously, most women of this type were compelled to seek employment outside the home to supplement their family income. Unlike their better off counterparts in the city, they did not seek work because of boredom or loneliness.

Now in order to determine whether a pregnant woman is 'at risk', the anganwadi worker would have to use a chart or list of risk factors. The preparation of such a chart or list of risk factors is an important task which can be accomplished by specialists in social obstetrics. Such work has been accomplished by their counterparts in other countries. For example, in the Ukranian SSR, the specialists in social obstetrics have prepared a list of two groups of factors that caused perinatal pathology. prenatal affecting a woman during pregnancy and intranatal during labour. Prenatal factors are divided into five subgroups. The first embraces social and biological factors such as the age of a mother or father, their family status, hazardous occupations, bad habits, a low cultural level and emotional stresses. The second sub-group comprises risk factors discovered during compiling a patient's anamenasis. These are: intervals between labours, previous abortions, premature labour, still birth, neonatal death, the birth of an abnormal baby with congenital anomalies, low or excessive birth weights, severe complications after previous labour, infertility for more than two or five years or gynaecological diseases. The third subgroup includes extragenital disorders; cardiovascular, hepatic, renal or endocrinic ailments, acute or chronic infections. Especially dangerous for a pregnant woman are cardiovascular diseases with disturbed blood circulation, hypertension, endocrinic disorders (diabetes) and various infections affecting the foetal egg. The fourth subgroup embraces complications of pregnancy: toxicosis, hemorrhage in the first and second halves of pregnancy; hydramnion, ocigoamnion, multiple pregnancy, pelvic presentation, overdue pregnancy, a risk of miscarriages. Severe late toxicosis, incompatibility of the mother and foetus's blood groups and Rh factor are regarded as factors causing the highest risk of perinatal pathology. The fifth subgroup includes different disorders during the intratubal development of the foetus (hypotrophy, fetal hypoxia, etc.) or in the foetus-placenta system. In all 52 prenatal pathology risk factors and 20 intranatal risk factors were identified[1]. A simplified list of risk factors can help the anganwadi worker in identifying pregnant women who would need special care and attention. The 'strategy of risk' used by obstetricians and paediatricians there consisted in the identification of risk factors, the determination of an influence they may produce on the outcome of pregnancy as well as in providing special medical care. All women without risk factors were required to undergo medical check-up at a clinic in the second half of pregnancy once a month and, after twenty weeks, twice a month. But if a women had one or more risk factors, she was examined more often depending upon her physical condition. Thus, like the medicine kit, a 'risk factors list' can be another very useful aid with the anganwadi workers to win over the confidence of pregnant women in the community and thereby enhance her credibility. This may also provide her an opportunity to refer complicated cases to the health centre for prompt attention. And if the health centre organises a special referral counter to deal with cases referred by the anganwadi worker, the entire complexion of the health situation of pregnant women (maternal mortality is as high as 340 in 1991)[2] can be changed for the better without involving any additional financial expenditure. By using this approach in the educational programme of pregnant women, a good foundation can be laid for the development of the children, an important objective of the ICDS programme.

It may be clarified that planning for health and nutrition education for pregnant woment is a process in which goals are set, educational methods and resources chosen and evaluation defined. For instance, educational requirements of grassroots level workers may include training in community organization, community participation, social and cultural aspects of health and nutrittion, the team approach and techniques of the communication. Health and nutrition education for the community as a whole is another important consideration which has a bearing on the education of women in general, and pregnant women, in particular. Educational efforts among the target population can be directed towards: (i) increasing awareness of community about pregnancy-related health and nutrition problems; (ii) preventing pregnancy-related health and nutrition problems; (iii) increasing the acceptance, support and use of services provided under the ICDS programme; and (iv) recruiting women volunteers and training them for development work in their respective areas.

THE MODEL

A model for planning health and nutrition education for

pregnant women has been developed here keeping in view the need to initiate child development, right from the time of conception. (See Appendix 6) As mentioned before, the focus is on the pregnant women because they play a crucial role in the development of their children. The need for giving greater importance to the pregnant women has been increasingly stressed in medical circles.

This model is a mechanism for defining the educational processes necessary for health and nutrition education of pregnant women. It can be a useful tool to be used by the anganwadi workers and their supervisors who are responsible for providing health and nutrition education to pregnant women. The purpose of providing health and nutrition education is to bring about improvement in the health and nutritional status of pregnant women. The model is not an end in itself rather it is a means by which a pregnant woman at risk can be identified and appropriate health and nutritional care provided. The model presents a step-by-step procedure, representing a comprehensive and inter-disciplinary approach to analysing problems of health and nutritional needs of pregnant women in different ICDS project areas. Basically, the model deliniates five steps :

(i) identification of health and nutritional problems of pregnant women as well as their needs for education in this regard ;

(ii) establishment of objectives to identify health and nutritional problems of pregnant women ;

(iii) selection of appropriate methods for attaining the objectives ;

(iv) implementing the health and nutrition education programme of pregnant women ; and

(v) evaluation.

These five aspects or steps of the interrelated process should normally be included in every effective plan for developing health and nutrition education programme. Implementation of this model, however, will depend on such factors as :

(i) identification of situations or entry points for providing health and nutrition education ;

(ii) attitudes and knowledge of the anganwadi workers, who will be solely responsible for providing health and nutrition education ;

(iii) supportive supervision from their middle-level staff like the mukhiya sevikas and the lady health visitors ; and

(iv) administrative support from the higher level ICDS planners and their facilitators.

The following steps need to be taken :

Step I--Identify the health and nutrition education needs of the pregnant women.

Identification of health and nutritional problems of pregnant women as well as their health and nutrition education needs is necessary from the consideration of implementing the ICDS programme. The health and nutrition education programme, in particular, will be largely shaped by the needs of the pregnant women and the knowledge and skills of providers of educational messages. As providers, the anganwadi workers have to understand clearly the relevant health and nutrition education processes. Actually, identification of health and nutritional needs of pregnant women begins with an understanding of their specific situations, particularly, the relationship of their health and nutritional beliefs and practices with their environment—physical, biologic and social. An understanding of the differences in pregnant women's knowledge, beliefs and practices would be necessary for laying adequate stress in the educational approach where it is most needed. The 'priority approach' like the 'risk approaeh' can be cost-effective, yielding maximum benefit to the pregnant women exposed to the health and nutrition education programme. In fact, development of a culturally-relevant health and nutrition education programme for pregnant women would require a thorough knowledge of their health and nutritional beliefs and practices; their present way of tackling their health and nutritional problems; and the kind of constraints they have faced in dealing with them in the past. Knowledge will also be needed about the relationship of their health and nutritional problems with their environment, especially in the domestic, health, social and economic spheres. A knowledge of their perceptions of dealing with these probiems can help a great deal in understanding what knowledge and skills the pregnant women will need to obtain maximum benefit from the educational programme. These goals serve to establish a common understanding of the aims and objectives of health and nutrition education among the beneficiaries and the providers. An adequate understanding about the misconceptions of pregnant women can be of tremendous help in dealing with those aspects which are relatively easy to handle. We had, in an earlier publication, high-lighted the importance of differentiating between the 'central' and 'peripheral' health and nutrition beliefs in a rural setting and we have suggested that it will be desirable to first change those negative peripheral beliefs which are least likely to be resisted by the people.[3] The central beliefs are hard to change. Similarly, in regard to the role performance of traditional birth attendants, we have suggested that first we should try to strengthen their 'positive beliefs' and then carefully attempt to discourage their negative beliefs. Incidentally, this model on the role of traditional birth attendants

(TBAs) has been highlighted in the Population Reports.[4] Unfortunately, in most training programmes of grassroots level workers, including the TBAs, and the AWWs, not much attention is paid to the people's beliefs since these are rarely identified. It is somewhat disheartening to note that in the widely-circulated text book of Preventive and Social Medicine, an example of a harmful belief about 'abortion due to eating of papaya' is repeated in every new edition of the book for the past few years, without ever caring to update the information. Obviously, there is a great need to have a countrywide classification of health and nutrition-related beliefs and practices of pregnant women. We may mention here that sometime back a federation of the Voluntary Associations of India had taken up this task but we are not aware whether all regions of the country have been covered. It may be worthwhile to mention here that the Aga Khan University in Karachi has made a good use of the 'cultural material', produced in India, in some of their training programmes for health workers.[5] An attempt has been made to update their 'data bank' on the health belief systems of the people. This is evident from some of their recent publications in a prestigious journal of 'Social Science and Medicine'. It may not be out of place to mention here that even a model about the delivery of health care services by different categories of health personnel, which has been proffered by us after years of painstaking research, has not been used in India in the planning of training programmes for health workers, despite the fact that it has been reproduced in a widely circulated foreign publication. Thus unless all the available information is put to proper use, howsoever hard we may try, we shall not be able to develop need-based training programmes for grassroots level health workers in our country. We may also mention that the manuals produced for the health workers are full of idealistic statements about "what to do" but without explaining as to 'how it can be done'. The gap between theory and practice, therefore, is too wide to be bridged easily.

Step II—Establish health and nutrition education goals for pregnant women.

This is dependent on a clear understanding of the health problems of pregnant women, their misconceptions, their fears, their prejudices, their beliefs and attitudes. In identifying their educational needs the type of intervention and information that all pregnant women need to know should be eonsidered. For example, pregnant women who are anaemic would need to know what all they should do in their situation to get rid of this condition. They would like to know the period for which they would need to take iron tablets, with or without iron-rich vegetables available to them, and also about the place from where they can get their supply of iron tablets uninterrupted. They would also need to know what changes in their diets and habit patterns can help them in this regard. In addition, they would need to know whether overconsumption of iron tablets will be harmful. Such questions are generally put by them to health workers. Similarly, they would have many queries about their work at home as well as in the field or in other settings with a view to finding out what type of work and also what work-load would be conducive to different stages of pregnancy. They would require information on food prescriptions and food proscriptions during all stages of pregnancy. Awareness of the nature and extent of such problems is necessary for planning health and nutrition education programmes for pregnant women. As health and nutrition education programme is a continuing and evolving process, the responsibility for covering specific aspects should be delegated to different personnel at different levels. At the health centre level, it should be the responsibility of all medical officers. On the other hand, at the subcentre level, it should be the resposibility of ANMs, while at the community level, it has to be the responsibility of AWWs. The specific goals of the educational programme, therefore, should be clearly understood by all concerned. Unless all those involved in this activity work as an integrated them, the transformation process of the country-side is bound to be slow.

Step III—Select appropriate educational methods

Appropriate educational methods can be identified only after formulating the educational goals based on the assessment of the needs of the pregnant women. The process of selecting educational methods should be a cooperative venture with the full participation of all members of the team, especially those at the grassroots level—the anganwadi workers. Actually, the educational messages should be thoroughly pretested before finalising them. Selecting educational methods that are culturally—relevant and appropriate involves identifying opportunities and situations for health and nutrition education of pregnant women for each of the goals. For identifying appropriate opportunities and situations, care should be taken to keep in mind the varied socioeconomic situations of the pregnant women. Decisions would be required to determine which situations or opportunities should be used, which techniques are best, and whether the method should be individual or group or a combination. Priorities can then be decided about the training procedure. For instance, at the anganwadi level, a group method involving interaction between the anganwadi worker, ANM and several pregnant women, may be more useful. On the other hand, ai the family level, an individual method involving anganwadi worker and a pregnant woman, may prove beneficial. Group methods can be used by the supervisors of the anganwadi worker, at the anganwadi level. At times, opportunities for health and nutrition education of pregnant women may occur during home visits by the anganwadi workers. Many other occasions may provide similar opportunities. Thus the more the contact with the community, the greater the possibility for interaction between the anganwadi workers and pregnant women. Criteria for the final selection of educational methods as usual must include effectiveness, efficiency, adequacy, and appropriateness. In the present context, effectiveness would mean the extent to which a defined activity achieves the goal. Only when the activity attains its goal, can one say that the educational method employed was effective. On the other hand, efficiency would be determined basically by assessing the amount of resources used to attain the goal. Important factors to be considered in this regard include manpower, time, material, and finance. Keeping in view the paucity of resources, only that activity which uses the least amount of resources to attain the goal can be considered as efficient. For example, use of cheap material produced locally would be more cost-effective than the material supplied from the city. As for adequacy, it reflects the degree to which an educational activity can achieve the goal. This is specially relevant to the ICDS programme. For example, as an activity, growth monitoring by itself may be quite inadequate. But when it is combined with an educational message, explaining how to improve the nutritional status of a child, a synergistic effect would occrue emphasising the value of combining one activity with another. Actually, this approach supports the concept of providing a package of integrated services under the ICDS programme. Lastly, appropriateness would indicate whether the method used was relevant to the specific culture or ecological situation of the pregnant women. Many a time, educational messages failed to convey the intended meaning. For example, referring a pregnant woman to a primary health centre for medical examination by a lady doctor without knowing anything about the availability of such a functionary at the health centre would mean misguiding the concerned pregnant woman. Sometimes, the recipients' perception of a given situation or concept may be totally different from that of the communicators. Consider for example, the tribal group in Mexico that was exposed to a series of slides showing the mosquitoes responsible for causing malaria. And later when the tribals were asked for their reactions, they just laughed and stated that "this kind of mosquitoes may be your problem because the size of our mosquitoes is very small". It would be useful, therefore, to use only those concepts which make sense to the people. Use of folk media like puppet shows and proverbs etc. might be more useful. Selecting appropriate educational methods is not an easy task even in the best of circumstances. The ' trainers" should therefore, possess certain basic knowledge and skills. They must also possess other characteristics such as (i) faith in the objectives of educational programmes (ii) willingness to help the weaker sections of the community, especially its vulnerable members, like pregnant women and children; (iii) a knowledge of educational processes and an ability to determine the types of situations that can be used to achieve different goals; and (iv) a knowledge of the health and nutritional beliefs and practices of the local people and also the ability to use every possible entry point for delivering the appropriate messages; and (v) a knowledge of the community resources and the ability to used them effectively.

It may be mentioned that flexibility of approach would be essential for the implementation of the educational programme. For example, collecting a group of pregnant women and exposing them to a stereotype lecture on health and nutritional problems will have little impact. But when the messages are given with the aid of culturally acceptable channels of communications, the impact is bound to be much greater. In the field situation, the limitations of the anganwadi workers must not be lost sight of. Overestimating their potentials would be as much a mistake as underestimating them.

Step IV—Carry out the Educational Programme.

The educational programme should be carried out as far as possible in accordance with the laid down objectives.

Step V—Evaluate health and nutrition education programme.

Since improvement in the health and nutritional level of

the pregnant women is the primary goal of the educational task within each setting, the major focus of evaluation should be related to the increment in the knowledge the pregnant woman shows as a result of the nutrition education programme as well as the adoption of healthful practices and use of available nutritious food. It is necessary, therefore, that we have measurable goals rather than having those goals which appear idealistic and cannot be easily measured. For example, a goal such as educating the pregnant woman merely to eat more to become healthy would be beyond measurement. On the other hand, a well defined goal such as to get rid of anaemia by using iron tablets, would be more amenable to measurement. It is necessary, therefore, that each goal should be 'critically'' examined and evaluated from time to time so as to have a 'good fit' with the changing situation of pregnant women. It might be profitable to take into consideration the varied family situations of pregnant women so that goals once reached are maintained by the pregnant women with the help of their own family members. In fact there should be constant evaluation of questions asked by the pregnant women and the answers given by the anganwadi workers. The entire educational programme should be constantly reviewed by a joint health-cum-social welfare team. If required, additional help can be sought from the available specialists in each ICDS project area. In the final analysis, evaluation of the impact of the health and nutrition education programme should be considered as an important component of the ICDS programme.

REFERNCES

1. Lukyanoya, E.M., et at (1986) Protection of Children's Health in the Ukrainian SSR, Zdorovya Publishers, USSR.

2. The State of World's Children (1991). The United Nations Childrens Fund (UNICEF), Oxford University Press.

3. Kakar, D.N. (1977) Fol and Modern Medicine—A North Indian Case Study. New Asian Publishers, New Delhi.

4. Traditional Midwives and Family Planning (1980) Population Reports Series J. No. 22,

5. Mull, D.S. (1991) Traditional Perceptions of Marasmus in Pakistan. Social Science and Medicine Vol. 32; No. 2, pp 175-191.

7

Community Participation in ICDS

Theoretically, participation means 'getting involved or being allowed to become involved in a decision making process or the delivery of a service or the evaluation of a service, or even simply to become one of a number of people consulted on an issue or a matter'[1]. It is important to pinpoint that 'participation is generally held to be good for the participants and of benefit to those making decision'. To be more precise, 'participation is seen as 'a way of broadening the range of inputs to a decision'.[2] Participation, therefore, is expected to make a difference, and is not simply to become a process of co-option. What needs to be understood is that participation may be desired by different people for different reasons. And the motivations for participation may vary from one setting to another. For the implementation of a programme like the ICDS, therefore, one has to be very careful in evolving the criteria for choosing participants. Participation of relevant members of the community can certainly make a big difference in the implementation of the ICDS programme. Way back, while discussing participation in health programmes, Peter Pritchard addressed the fundamental question "Why participate at all ?" He felt that there were a range of advantages to membrrs of the community and to doctors' clients, in particular, a sense of contribution, a feeling of some power or place in the system, the spread of information throughout the community, and a willingness to be prepared and to support a negotiated allocation of resources for health care. Pritchard was of the view that 'the practice of medical care is improved because participation provides feedback from clients to the practitioners and the health-care staff, facilitiates and supports self-help groups, and, in particular, improves communication, job satisfaction and minimises the number of complaints[3]'. He was also of the view that 'participation lessens professional and technical domination of health care, helps the bureaucracy to respond to change, and brings about a more appropriate allocation of resources, particularly scarce health-care resources in society at large[4]'. Pritchard goes on to discuss the important role envisaged for community participation in health as a result of the Alma-Ata Declaration. In this participation, 'primary health care is the direct result of community activity and the local community takes an active, or even sponsoring role, so that locally derived priorities are served and local community resources used as far as possible'. According to Pritchard "The Alma-Ata statements on community participation are at the centre of professional values and beliefs and pose a threat[5]". This then is the nature of dialogue on community participation in social science circles. T.N. Madan, a reputed Indian sociologist, who has recently examined the role of community participation in health programmes has something interesting to state in this regard. He says, 'the only viable concept of community involvement is that which takes an 'incremental' view and seeks community cooperation in healאh schemes at the various stages of planning, implementation, and execution, but does not absolve the government of its ultimate responsibility for public health[6].

With this background in mind, we went ahead to find out the community's perception of the ICDS programme in our study area. We interviewed a group of 400 female respondents from the area served by the 20 selected anganwadis. The respondents were selected on a random basis and the majority of them were between the ages 26 and 35. Most of them were either illiterates or had studied upto the primary standard (71%). And the majority of them came from families with a monthly income of Rs. 1000 to Rs. 1500 (68%). They represented different castes but most of them came from nuclear families. (Table 32). It was interesting to know that most of them were

TABLE 32

Distribution of Respondents according to their Sociodemographic Characteristics

Characteristics	Rural Area No=200	Urban Slums No=200	Total No=400
I. Age Group (in year)			
(i) Below	13.0	7.5	10.2
(ii) 21—25	19.0	22.5	20.8
(iii) 26—30	27.0	25.5	26.2
(iv) 31—35	18.0	15.0	16.0
(v) 36 and above	23.0	28.5	26.2
II. Educational Status			
(i) Illiterate	53.0	10.0	31.5
(ii) Upto Primary	30.0	49.0	39.5

(iii) Upto Secandary	15.0	28.0	21.7
(iv) College and above	2.0	12.5	7.3
III. Caste Status			
(i) Upper castes	40.0	34.0	37.0
(ii) Middle castes	29.0	23.5	26.2
(iii) Lower and backward classes	31.0	42.5	36.8
IV. Family Income (In Rupees)			
Less than 1000	56.0	34.0	45.0
1001—1500	20.0	26.0	23.0
1501—2000	15.0	26.5	20.8
2001 and above	9.0	13.5	11.2
V. Family Type			
Joint/Extended	52.5	42.5	47.5
Nuclear	47.5	57.5	52.5

aware that an anganwadi was functioning in their area. However, only 48 percent of these respondents were eligible for the ICDS. And of them, only 71.3 percent had actually availed of the anganwadi services during the past one year. (Table 33-34) The most used services by them were : non-formal preschool education (75%) ; immunization (65%) ; and supplementary nutrition (63%). In contrast, the under-used services were : health check-up, growth monitoring, and medical aid (Table 35) We found that, on the whole, services like pre-school education and supplementary feeding were utilized more in rural areas than in urban slums. In contrast, services such as immunization,

TABLE 33

Distribution of Respondents according to their Knowledge about the Existence and Use of Anganwadi Services

Knowledge/Use of Anganwadi Services	Yes	No
(i) Knowledge of Anganwadi		
Rural Area	180 (90.0)	20 (10.0)
Urban Slums	148 (74.0)	52 (26.0)
(ii) Use of Services		
Rural Area	126 (70.0)	54 (30.0)
Urban Slums	108 (72.9)	40 (27.1)
Total	234 (71.3)	94 (28.7)

TABLE 34

Distribution of Respondents according to their Eligibility and Utilization of ICDS Services

Eligibility/Received	Yes	No
Eligibility of ICDS		
Rural	77 (37.1)	131 (62.9)
Urban	115 (49.8)	77 (40.2)
Total	192 (48.0)	208 (52.0)
Use of ICDS		
Rural	70 (63.6)	40 (36.4)
Urban	48 (58.5)	34 (41.4)
Total	118 (61.4)	74 (38.6)

TABLE 35

Distribution of Respondents according to their Present Use of Services Provided at the Anganwadi

Utilization of services	Rural Area No=70	Urban Slums No=48	Total No=118
(i) Non-formal pre-school education	61.7	38.3	75.4
(ii) Supplementary Nutrition	51.7	48.3	64.4
(iii) Immunization	46.6	53.4	63.5
(iv) Health check-up	46.2	53.8	55.1
(v) Growth monitoring	33.4	63.6	28.1
(vi) Medical Aid	54.2	45.8	35.6

health check-up and medical aid were utilized more in urban slums than in rural areas. Non-utilization or under-utitization of services was attributable to four factors : (i) inability to visit the anganwadi due to occupational pressure ; (ii) children were already going to a school ; (iii) unsuitable anganwadi timings ; and (iv) lack of variety in food preparations served at the anganwadi. Obviously, community participation in the ICDS programme was far from adequate. This aspect, therefore, deserves utmost attention in the ICDS circles. We hardly need to stress that without active community involvement or community participation, the ICDS programme cannot achieve its laid down objectives. Here we can learn a lot from the Chinese approach of seeking community participation for their development programmes. China has brought about a revolution in health care by laying a great stress on providing services to rural people. After the Great Proletarian Cultural Revolution, 70 percent of the State's funds for medical and health purposes were allocated to rural areas. As a result, 60 percent of the medical apparatuses were sent to the countryside. Simultaneously, the majority of medical graduates, throughout the country, were assigned work in rural areas. The State had increased the production of medicines, medical equipment and biological products to meet the needs of rural population. The prices of medicines were also reduced considerably. Another important aspect of the development of the health care system in China was that medical workers were encouraged to settle down in the countryside. This approach greatly helped in reinforcing their commune hospital staff. Yet another striking feature of the Chinese health care system was that medical and health departments were asked to run free health schools to train peasant doctors for the production brigades. In several production brigades, various forms of cooperative medicine were organized by the masses themselves. For example, in Chenkechuang peoples' Commune of Chuncheng country, of a total of 53 production brigades, as many as 30 practiced collective mutual aid and health care. The brigade organization and its members pooled funds for medicines and worked out a system of management. And all this happened in China hardly two decades ago when in 1970, Chairman Mao Tsetong, issued a special directive affirming cooperative medicine and barefoot doctors. The directive called on the whole country to popularise cooperative medicines promptly and make great effort to train barefoot doctors. Undoubtedly, the progress made in health care in China, has enormously fulfilled the wishes and the demands of the peasant masses. We may give here just one example to stress this point. In Changwe Prefecture, a health network has been functioning successfully for a number of years. The system has been organized in such a way that the country hospitals are run by the people's government and the Commune health centres by the Government subsidy. But the Brigade Cooporative Medical Services is collectively run by the members of the Brigade themselves. Another remarkable aspect of the Chinese health care system is that each production team has its own health workers who help the brigade barefoot doctors in organising the masses for the prevention of diseases and treatment of minor ailments and injuries[7]. Thus the basic units of the health network in China are the Brigade clinics—the principal organizational form of the cooperative medical system. However, the most important aspect of the Chinese health care system is that it is based on voluntary participation. (See Appendix 7 for India—China comparison on selected variables).

For implementing the ICDS programme, therefore, we should not forget Chairman Mao's words that "new things always have to experience difficulties and setbacks as they grow". The ICDS progremme can serve its purpose only when the people themselves will realize that it is a reliable guarantee of health and wellbeing of their children and other vulnerable members of their community. Only then would they be willing to come forward to support the programme, cherish it, and consider it their moral duty to develop it further. Ultimately, our policy should be to entrust the task of running the Anganwadis to the community itself. The community may decide to ask the elected panchayat members to set up a Child Development Committee (CDC) of dedicated persons to look after the anganwadi with regard to its democratic management and performing such tasks as raising funds for purchase of need-based medicines, maintenance of the anganwadi building, arrangement of food for supplementary feeding, payment of stipends to anganwadi workers and helpers etc. The CDC may decide giving specific responsibility to individual members keeping in view their special interests and potentials. But the CDC should take the full responsibility for settling all accounts of the anganwadi expenditure preferablyon a monthly basis. Ultimately, all rules and regulations in regard to the implementation of the ICDS programme should be drawn up and enforced through mass discussions and consensus. To be precise, the problem of raising funds for the anganwadi may have to be discussed with the people to seek their suggestions. This way alone, the ICDS scheme can be placed under mass supervision. With an eye on getting prompt results in curing diseases, tackling childhood malnutrition, helping pregnant women and lactating mothers and providing informal education to preschool children, the CDC can adopt a mutally acceptable approach to tap all possible resources for running the anganwadis. This way, a group from within the community, may play the role of a catalytic agent and bring about the desired change in regard to integrated child development. In fact, with the help of representatives of health and social welfare departments, the CDC could decide its own priorities. For instance, the CDC may decide and advocate the policy of laying greater stress on prevention rather than cure. The CDC may ask and encourage the anganwadi workers and the auxiliary nurse-midwives to jointly organize special health campaigns with a view to improving the hygiene of children and their mothers, of ensuring availability of safe drinking-water to them ; of looking after the drainage system ; or of removing the mosquito breeding centres. The CDC's empasis may be on preventing the oecurrence of the disease in the first place rather than curing it after in has occurred, as it often happens in our country. Improving the environment would mean cutting down the incidence of communicable diseases. We have pointed out elsewhere that most commonly prevalent diseases are environmental in origin[8-10]. The CDC could certainly play a crucial role in mobilising and organising the masses for the prevention and treatment of commonly prevalent diseasses. The CDC may even encourage the use of folk media like folk songs, puppet shows, 'nautanki' etc. to teach the community basic things such as, how to eliminate pests, insects, mosquitoes etc. and this way change their unhealthy and unhygienic habits. But it may be a good idea, to include some female members in the CDC. In any case, we should not lose sight of the long-term objectives of the ICDS scheme, that is, initiation of a process of social change – a process which can be sustained only by the communities concerned through their own understanding, involvement, and cooperation. It is therefore necessary to understand what community members themselves feel about the ICDS programme. Do they think they were given an opportunity to become aware of its benefits for their children ? Do they think they have a contribution to make towards its success ? Do they think that this programme too will meet the fate of its predecessors ? And, do they think that all is well with the programme as long as someone else is the 'giver', and they, the takers ? Obviously, awareness on the part of some members of the community about the existence of an anganwadi in their area is not enough. These members too need to understand its usefulness before they can associate with it or treat it as their own. It may not be out of place to mention here that under the Johns Hopkins University sponsored health projects in rural Punjab (1962-1973), an innovative strategy was adopted for securing community participation in health programmes. When for instance, it was discovered that a large number of malnourished children, representing the poorer sections of the community required supplementary feeding and care, a decision was taken, with the full understanding and cooperation of the Panchayat members, to open a day care centre in the village.

Their help was sought for (i) securing a centrally-located building for the day care centre; (ii) obtaining wheat for preparing a mid-day meal for children, and (iii) motivating working mothers to send their malnourished children to the day care centre. On one occasion certain vested interests in the village deliberately tried to spread numours about the quality of medical care being provided by a resident auxiliary nurse-midwife. The project social scientist came to her rescue in no time. The source of rumours was traced to a local quack who felt threatened by her presence. The issue was resolved with the help of village leaders with whom he had a good rapport.

We hardly need to emphasise that thousands of children in Chandigarh today live in an impoverished environment. They come from poor families. Their parents are steeped in illogical beliefs and superstitions. Their development is affected by a host of interacting factors, ranging from poor family income to inaccessibility of health, nutrition and educational facilities. They are obviously in need of help. And the ICDS programme is meant to help them in their predicament. The million-dollar question is : how to make people take full advantage of the ICDS programme ? Also, how to make them realize that, in the long run, they themselves would need to take greater responsibility for the development and well-being of their children. At the present juncture, their active participation in the ICDS programme can be beneficial in many ways, the predominant being in cutting down the operational cost of the programme, aimed at improving the health and nutritional status of their children. From the cost-benefit viewpoint, the returns have to be convincting enough to justify extension of the programme to other areas. The best we can do in these circumstances is to acquaint the anganwadi workers with certain basic principles of securing community participation. In this connection, we may mention here that in a manual entitled 'Practical Mother and Child Health Care (1979) produced by Drs. B.N.S. Walia, P.M. Shah and Kusum Shah, the then Group Convenors for the ICDS for several states, including Haryana, Punjab, Gujarat and Maharashtra, we had discussed certain basic principles for securing community participation in MCH programme by health workers.[11] We proffer here some practical ways of securing community participation in the ICDS programme by the anganwadi workers. In our opinion if the anwanwadi workers adopt these principles, their task of securing community participation in the ICDS programme could become a lot more easier.[12] (Appendix 8).

REFERENCES

1. Brownlea, A. (1987) Participation, Myths, Realities and Prognosis. Social Science and Medicine, Vol. 25, No. 6, pp. 605-614.
2. *Ibid*
3. Pritchard, P. (1986) Why participate at all ? In primary Health Care 2000 (Edited by Fry J and Hasler J) Chap. 7. Churchill Livingstone, London.
4. *Ibid*
5. *Ibid*
6. Madan, T.N. (1987) Community Involvement in Health Policy. Sociostructural and Dynamic Aspects of Health Beliefs. Soc. Sci. Med. Vol. 25, No. 6, pp. 615-620.
7. Cheng. Wei (1978) Cooperative Medieal Service, Foreign Language Press, Peking, China.
8. Kakar, D.N. (1988) Primary Health Care and Traditional Medical Practitioners, Sterling Publishers, New Delhi.

9. Kakar D.N. Chopra S. (1990) Environmental Factors Affecting Health in an Urban Slum. In : The New Environmental Age (Editors R.K. Sapru and Shyama Bhardwaj) Ashish Publishing House, New Delhi.

10. Kakar, D.N. (1991) Poverty among Harijans : A Study of Causative Factors. In : Social Science Research and Problem of Poverty (Ed. Tarlok Singh) Concept Publishing Company, New Delhi.

11. Walia, B.N.S., Shah, P.M., and Shah, Kusam (1979) Practical Mother and Child Health Care, Orient Longman Limited, Bombay.

12. Kakar, D.N. (1979) How to get Community Participation in an acceptable way. In Practical Mother and Child Health Care. (Eds. Walia, B.N.S., et al) Orient Longman Limited, Bombay.

8

Conclusions and Recommendations

CONCLUSIONS :

Based on our studies, the following conclusions are proffered :

I. that the ICDS scheme in Chandigarh is a befitting response to the needs of thousands of children who are malnourished and who live in an impoverished environment. It needs to be recognized that it is not only in the so-called BIMARU States (U.P., Bihar, Rajasthan, Madhya Pradesh and Andhra Pradesh) that the basic services for children are deficient. Even in Chandigarh —the city beautiful—there are BIMARU areas such as urban slums and villages where health and social services for children are still quite inadequate—they are poorly, manned, underfinanced, and inaccessible to underprivileged sections of the community.

II. that till 1978, when there was no ICDS scheme in Chandigarh, no development or health agency had taken the responsibility for guarnteeing that all children below six years should receive a package of services on integrated development.

III. that the physical environment of the anganwadis studied by us is far from satisfactory, especially, in terms of the conditions of the anganwadi buildings and provision of certain basic facilities such as a toilet, and a container for keeping drinking water.

IV. that the anganwadi workers are inadequately trained and supported for performing certain important tasks such as (i) home visiting; (ii) identifying pregnant women at risk ; (iii) identifying children with physical and mental disorders and (iv) diagnosing and treating their minor ailments.

V. that the present system of using a referral slip for referring acute cases for medical attention is highly deficient because it does not provide a feedback to the anganwadi workers.

VI. that the majority of the anganwadi workers have made good adjustment on the role assigned to them as is reflected by the years of service they have put in. Even those coming from outside the villages have found it convenient attend to their duties religiously. Nevertheless, they are feeding themselves on the hope of getting a better honrarium and becoming 'permanent' in the near future.

VII. That there is no evidence of community participation in the ICDS programme—an aspect which deserves to be given the top priority. and,

VIII. that as yet no studies on the social aspects of the ICDS scheme are available. This is surprising because while many social scientists seem committed to an assault on poverty, none appears to be concerned about studying the ICDS seheme.

RECOMMENDATIONS :

1. The children belonging to the disadvantaged groups deserve many advocates to represent them and their needs to the society so that programmes and serviccs aimed at integrated child development are available in every nook and corner of our society.

2. The ICDS scheme should be made more realistic and flexible in ways that will genuinely strengthen not only the individual child but also its home and family—the two important determinants of child development.

3. One of the major thrusts of the ICDS scheme should be to train the anganwadi workers well enough to identify physical disorders in the earliest years of life—ages one through three years—because if these are treated in time, many of their adverse consequences can be avoided.

4. The 'strategy of risk' should be developed in such a way that the anganwadi worker is well equipped in detecting the risk factors that can influence the outcome of pregnancy. She should be helped in planning a nutrition education programme for pregnant women.

5. One of the aims of home visiting should be to determine the physical condition of pregnant women, to teach them the hygiene of pregnancy, to prepare them for childbirth and to instruct them how to behave after it, especially in terms of getting the child immunized against preventable diseases. Another aim of home

visiting should be to inform the parents about how to identify signs and symptoms of commonly prevalent childhood illnesses and to teach them about the measures that should be taken to eliminate these. In fact, the major task should be the dissimination of hygienic knowledge among the population and inculcation of hygienic habits in parents so that the necessary conditions for integrated child development are created.

6. Women belonging to the disadvantaged sections of the community must be provided with full information about the work opportunity so that they could volunteer themselves for the available positions.

7. Understandably, there is no dearth of information indicating that poverty and inequality tend to adversely affect the physical, intellectual, emotional, and social development of children. Yet more detailed research is needed on the effects of these two variables in defferent rural and urban settings. The focus of such research should be on (i) the differential impact of poverty and inequality on children of different caste groups and (ii) on the differential impact of socialising agents such as anganwadi workers and the auxiliary nurse midwives on children in different caste groups.

8. Regular supervision, democratic and informal staff meetings, opportunities for joint work, especially visits to the homes of the beneficiaries are essential for efficient working of the ICDS system, in general, and intersectoral collaboration, in particular.

9. The training of anganwadi workers should cover aspects sucd as (a) child development from a holistic viewpoint so as to promote an undertaking of the devices, conflicts and capacities, characteristic of successive stages

of learning; (b) practical approaches of dealing with a wide range of behavioural problems of children so that more children eould be enrolled at the anganwadis; (c) provision of skills which can help anganwadi workers to deal effectively with the life stresses which destroy the underprivileged child's ability to participate in the programs and activities of the anganwadi; and (d) ways of tackling other identifiable problems of children.

10. Training of trainers should be given the top priority. The Child Development Project Officer and other senior level functionaries should receive training in some basic aspects of child development such as motor, emotional, social, intellectual, moral and motivational aspects. They should also get training on culture-specific and age-specific problems and needs of children. Such training will help in enhancing their sensitivity to possible disorderded patterns of child development. Mukhya Sevika and Auxiliary Nurse Midwives should also be trained in these aspects so that they become sensitive to distortions in child development.

11. The physical environment of the anganwadis and the working conditions of the anganwadi workers should be improved by adopting the following measures :

    (i) Granting them fringe benefits such as free medical leave, earned leave and maternity leave.

    (ii) Providing toilet facilities at the anganwadis.

    (iii) Providing one supervisor for 8-10 anganwadis.

    (iv) Simplifying the recording system.

    (v) Providing opportunities to the anganwadi workers for participation in seminars and conferences related to the ICDS scheme.

    (vi) Organising refresher courses and special lectures covering medical aspects as well as the cultural context of health and nutrition ;

(vii) Encouraging the anganwadi workers to supplement family income by participation in income-generating activities.

(viii) Providing substitutes for anganwadi workers during leave periods.

(ix) Promoting channels of communication so that they can discuss their problems freely with their seniors;

(x) Reviewing their workload periodically so that they are not burdened.

12. Each village and urban slum with an anganwadi should have a Child Development Committee (CDC) to help in the planning and execution of various activities of the ICDS scheme. The anganwadi worker should seek community participation in a planned way.

Appendix I

Sex-wise distribution of population covered under the two ICDS projects in Chandigarh

Sex	Project I		Project II		Total	
	No	%	No	%	No	%
Male	52342	54.2	55, 455	54.9	1, 07, 797	54.6
Female	44284	45.8	45, 546	45.1	89, 830	45.4
Total	96, 626	100.0	1, 01, 101	100.0	1, 97, 627	100.0

Appendix II

Agewise distribution of children covered under the two ICDS Projects in Chandigarh.

Projects	Age Group				Total
	Below 6 months	6 months to 1 years	1 year to 3 years	3 years to 6 years	
Project I	1628	2102	4838	8825	17, 393
Project II	1896	2353	5009	9962	19, 220
Total	3, 524	4, 455	9, 847	18, 787	36, 613

Appendix III

Age-wise distribution of children receiving supplementary nutrition under the ICDS Projects in Chandigarh.

	6 months to 3 yrs.			1 yrs.-3 yrs.		3-6 years			
Children	Project I	Project II	Total	Project I	Project II	Total	Project I	Project II	Total
Number of children	1414	1738	3152	3308	4194	7502	8544	9962	18506
Number of children enrolled	701	626	1327	2223	2136	4359	3918	4253	8171
Number of children who received SNP for 15 days or more	628	552	1180 (37.4)	2154	1954	4108 (54.7)	3675	3543	7218 (39.00)
	2743	2916	5659	7685	8284	1569	16137	11758	33895

Appendix IV

Distribution of Pregnant women and lactating mothers covered under the two ICDS Projects

Type of women	Pregnant		Lactating		Total	
	Project I	Project II	Project I	Project II	Pregnant	Lactating
1. Total number of eligible women in the area	1280	1687	1346	1896	2967	3242
2. Total number of women enrolled	950	1070	1063	1146	2020	2209
3. Total number of women who received SNP for 15 days or more.	902	894	1000	992	1796	1992

Appendix V

Age-wise distribution of children according to their nutritional status covered under the two ICDS Projects in Chandigarh.

Nutritional status	Age Group	
	One to three years	Three to six years
Normal	787	2704
Grade I	541	2242
Grade II	297	1062
Grade III	19	17
Grade IV	2	–
Total	1646	6025

Source: Appendices 1 to V are based on CDPO's monthly progress report for the month of October, 1991.

Appendix VI

A model for Planning Health and Nutrition Education for Pregnant Women by Anganwadi Worker.

1	2	3	4	5
Identify health and nutrition education needs of pregnant women	Set health and nutrition education goals for pregnant women	Select appropriate methods to meet each health and nutrition education goals for pregnant women	Carry out health and nutrition education programme	Evaluate health and nutrition education of pregnant women 1. To what extent methods chosen for health and nutrition education were approved and efficient?
Determine health and Nutrition education needs of	Assess prablems in reaching each goal	Determine Situations and entry points for health and		

(*Contd.*)

1	2	3	4	5
pregnant women		nutrition education for each of the goals		2. To what extent were health education needs of pregnant women adequately identified.
Determine to what extent pregnant women possess knowledge about Relevant health and nutrition concepts	Review possible health and nutrition education goals for pregnant women Decide on short-term and long-term health and nurtition education goals Determine priority of goals	Review possible methods for reaching	Determine specifically what health and nutrition education is to be imparted by AWW, where, when and how	3. To what extent were nutrition education needs of pregnant women adequately identified.
Determine				

(*Contd.*)

1	2	3	4	5
health and nutrition education goals from view-point of pregnant women		each health and nutrition education goals		4. To what extent were knowledge of pregnant women about health and nutritional concepts adequately assessed. 5. To what extent were health and nutrition education goals realistic and timely. 6. To what extent were goals given the best priority.

Appendix VII

A Comparative Picture of India and China giving Information on Selected Indicators of Relevance to ICDS (1991)*

Basic	1	2	3	4	5	6	7	8	9	10
Indicators	Total population (millions) 1989	Life expectancy at birth (years) 1989	GNP per capita (US $) 1988 1985	Total adult literacy rate 1985	% of age group enrolled in primary school total 1986-1988	Under 5 mortality rate 1960-1989	Infant mortality rate (under 1) 1960-1989	Annual no of births (thousands) 1989	Annual no. of under 5 deaths (thousands) 1989	Maternal Mortality Rate
India	835.6	59	340	44	98	282 145	165 96	26071	3780	340
China	1122.4	70	330	68	132	203 43	150 31	24580	1057	44

Nutrition	1	2		3	4	5
	% of infants with low birth-weight 1980-88	No. of children (1980-89) suffering from under weight (0-4 years)		Average index of food production per capita 1979-80=100	Daily per capita caloric supply as % of requirements	% of household income (1980-85) spent on all food
		Moderate and Severe	Severe	1989	1984-86	
India	30	41	6	118	100	52
China	9	21	3	129	111	61

	% of population with access to safe water 1985-88			Percentage fully immunised 1981/88-89 one-year old children					ORT use rate 1987-88
	Total	Urban	Total	TB	DPT	Polio	Measles	Pregnant Women Tetanus	
India	57	76	50	12/89	31/83	7/82	-/69	24/69	23
China	—	85	—	-/98	-/95	-/96	-/95	—	30

Health	1		2		3			
Education	Adult literacy rate				Primary school enrolment ratio			
	1970		1985		1960 (gross)		1986.88 (gross)	
	Male	Female	Male	Female	Male	Female	Male	Female
India	47	20	58	29	80	40	113	81
China	—	—	80	55	—	—	140	124

*Modified from the State of World's Children, UNICE (1991).

Appendix VIII

Practical ways of securing community participation by the anganwadi worker.

1. Interact freely with all people regardless of their caste status

The anganwadi worker can establish a good rapport with the pregnant women, lactating mothers and families of children attending the anganwadi only when she takes them into full confidence. If she approaches them in a friendly way, she is bound to secure a positive response from them. Afterall, she dresses like them, speaks the same language, and is a product of the same culture.

2. Avoid identification with any faction

The anganwadi worker can maintain consistent progress in her work only when she keeps good relations with all sections of the community without identifying herself with any faction. Sometimes grassroots level workers unconsciously identify themselves with a powerful faction in the community. This can have an adverse effect on the programme. The success of the ICDS programme will greatly depend on her good relationships with all members of the community.

3. Identify and appreciate local beliefs and practices which are beneficial

The anganwadi worker can play a vital role in imparting health and nutrition education to pregnant women and lactating mothers by encouraging those beliefs and practices that are beneficial to their health. At the same time, she need not bother about beliefs and practices which are neither benificial nor harmful. But she must take utmost care in discouraging the harmful beliefs and practices.

4. Identify problems and tackle them jointly with the beneficeries or their families

It would be better if the anganwadi worker discusses the problems faced by her in implementing the ICDS programme with the beneficaries or their families and then seek their support in solving them. Joint tackling of problems will go a long way in reaching the benefits of the ICDS programme to all concerned.

5. Keep a track of the referred cases to the health centre

The anganwadi worker can establish her credibility in the community by following up all cases referred by her to the health centre for medical attention. She should persuade her colleagues from the health department to open a special referral counter at the health centre.

6. Maintain liaison with all families in the community for establishing early contact with the pregnant women

The anganwadi worker can contribute maximally to child development through early contact with pregnant women and then providing them health and nutrition education in time. The effort should be to identify 'women at risk' at the earliest opportunity so that they could be provided prompt medical attention.

7. Seek the cooperation of village leaders

The anganwadi worker must maintain a good relationship with the village leaders like the panchyat members and seek their cooperation for better functioning of the ICDS programme. This will be possible only when she keeps them informed about all activities of the ICDS programme and also their benefits to the children.

8. Maintain spirits to present a good example

The anganwadi worker is bound to face many a bad moment in her day-to-day work. Now if she maintains her spirits even in the worst possible circumstances, she is bound to set up a good example for others to follow.